THE
SPIRIT-
FILLED
LIFE

TIMOTHY C. TENNENT

Printed in the United States of America

Cover design by Strange Last Name
Page design by PerfecType, Nashville, Tennessee

Tennent, Timothy C.
The Spirit-filled life / Timothy C. Tennent. – Frankin, Tennessee : Seedbed Publishing, ©2019.

pages ; cm

The contents of this work originated from a sermon series, of the same name, preached by the author at Asbury Theological Seminary, in 2019.
Includes bibliographical references
ISBN 9781628247824 (pbk. : alk. paper)
ISBN 9781628247831 (mobipocket ebk.)
ISBN 9781628247848 (epub ebk.)
ISBN 9781628247855 (updf ebk.)

1. Holy Spirit--Biblical teaching. 2. Spiritual life--Biblical teaching.
3. Spiritual formation. 4. Christian life--Methodist authors. I. Title.

BS680.H56.T46 2019   231/.3   2019949863

SEEDBED PUBLISHING
Franklin, Tennessee
seedbed.com

In honor of Arvid and Judy Metcalf,
two servants of God who daily demonstrate what
it means to live the Spirit-filled life.

Contents

CONTENTS

Introduction

Each year I write a small book to share with the friends of Asbury Seminary some teaching on a Christian theme. This has become a tradition at Asbury, dating back to our founder, H. C. Morrison, who published what, at that time, was known as the *Pentecostal Herald*, today known simply as *The Herald*. It has always been part of Asbury's mission to not just train future pastors and leaders who are preparing for ministry, but also to help train and equip all those who are connected to the larger ministry of Asbury Theological Seminary. You are an important part of our mission, and we see you as integral to the ministry and outreach of Asbury around the world.

The world cannot hear the message of Christ well if it is only heralded by a professional class of full-time ministers. It must be shared and embodied in and through the whole church. Every member has the privilege and responsibility to bear witness to the Christian gospel in both word and deed. However, many Christians feel inadequate and are not getting strong biblical teaching in their local church. They believe the gospel, but they do not know how to discover their own gifts, or do not always see how their lives can be used effectively for the extension of the good news of Jesus Christ. Perhaps you feel that way at times. We all need teaching that is practical, biblical, and reliable.

We asked many of you in recent years what questions you have, and how we can help you grow as a Christian. One of the prominent responses to that question was that many of you felt that you did not understand the role of the Holy Spirit in your life. You accepted Jesus and you understand the centrality of his death and resurrection in your life, but were not as confident about what happens after that. Central to the Christian message is that even after conversion, God continues to work in us and prepare us for effective witness. It is important to not just *become* a Christian, but to learn how to *live* as a Christian. This book is a response to that need.

This year I decided to preach a series of sermons at Asbury entitled "The Spirit-Filled Life." This book is taken from that series. It is my hope that each and every one who reads this book will grow in their Christian life, and become more aware of the amazing ministry of the Holy Spirit in our lives.

One

The Holy Spirit in the Old Testament

Scriptural Background: Isaiah 61:1–3;
Luke 3:21–22; 4:1–2, 14

When we think of the Holy Spirit, we often assume that the Holy Spirit comes to us on the day of Pentecost. If we take that assumption, we would make the New Testament, particularly the book of Acts, our starting point for understanding the Holy Spirit. However, this is not the case. The Holy Spirit is one of the members of the triune God and, therefore, we meet the Holy Spirit all through the Bible. Therefore, this book begins by a brief survey of the presence of the Holy Spirit with the Old Testament. There are so many texts I could choose from the Old Testament, but I've selected a few in order to give a picture of the full role of the Holy Spirit in the Old Testament. These are all chosen in order to paint a picture of the functions of the Holy Spirit.

Overview of the Holy Spirit in the Old Testament

When we open the Bible to Genesis, we immediately find the Holy Spirit hovering over the waters. He's right there in the act of creation. When we are created, God breathes into us *ruah*, the Hebrew word for the "breath of life," or "spirit"—used for your spirit, Holy Spirit, wind, and breath. This same word is used for all of those meanings based on the context. So here is the Father breathing into us the Spirit of God, and this is what makes us image-bearers. Later on, as the Israelites go into the wilderness, they attend a meeting about constructing the tabernacle, and they have to design a lot of new things. They have to design altars. They have to design basins, utensils, priestly clothing, candlesticks, and on and on it goes. They don't have the knowledge to do this. Now, apparently, Bezalel had the gifts for it, but he had no experience to know what to do. We're told in Exodus 31:1–3 that the Spirit of God came down on Bezalel so that he could make the things in the tabernacle.

In Numbers 11:25–26, the Spirit of God falls on the seventy elders at the tent of meeting, anointing them for leadership. But, the Spirit also fell on Eldad and Medad, two of the elders who were not present at the tent of meeting, but were in the main camp. Thus, there were seventy-two who were anointed, which is the number of the nations, the great anticipation of that theme of the Spirit being poured out on all peoples. In Deuteronomy 34:9, Moses lays his hands on Joshua and he prays that he be filled with the Spirit of God, that he might follow through on the ministry of Moses and lead as his successor.

In the book of Judges, there is a long sequence of examples where the Holy Spirit comes on the judges. The Holy Spirit falls on Gideon to defeat the Midianites (Judg. 6:34), on Jephthah to fight the Ammonites (Judg. 11:29), and on Samson to fight the Canaanites (Judg. 13:25). We see the Spirit of God coming on Saul to prophesy (1 Sam. 10:6), which is the sign that he had been chosen as the first king of Israel. David, also, is anointed with the Holy Spirit to lead Israel (1 Sam. 16:13), and the Spirit is withdrawn from Saul.

We also find a really remarkable passage in 2 Samuel 23:2 where David is at the end of his ministry. He's about to write a final hymn which will represent the last words of King David. He says something which should really grab your attention. He says that the words he is about to pen were given to him by the Holy Spirit. Now we know that 2 Peter 1:21 looks back on all the prophets and declares that they were all carried along by the Holy Spirit as they spoke from God. But here you have David's own self-declaration that God, through his Holy Spirit, has given him the words to speak. In 2 Kings 2:9, Elisha prays for a double portion of the Holy Spirit. Make that one of your prayers today.

In Job 33:4, Job is looking back and remembering the creation act in Genesis. And he explicitly says that when we were created, the Spirit of God breathed into us. He makes explicit what is clearly there in Genesis (see also Psalm 104:30). When you move into the book of Psalms, you may recall how the Holy Spirit appears in many of the psalms. For example, you have David's anguished prayer for sin in Psalm 51:11 where he says, "Take not thy Holy Spirit from me" (KJV). Or the prayer in Psalm 139:7 where David says, "Where can I go from your Spirit?" Those we know pretty well, but what about Psalm 106:33 where the history of Israel is recounted? The text does not say what you would expect: that they rebelled against the Lord. Instead, it says they rebelled against the Holy Spirit. And in Psalm 143:10, David prays for the Lord to lead him by the Holy Spirit on a level path.

In Isaiah 44:3, Isaiah speaks a prophecy that could have been proclaimed by Peter at Pentecost: "I will pour out my Spirit on your offspring, and my blessing on your descendants." And then there is Isaiah 61:1, quoted by Jesus: "The Spirit of the Sovereign LORD is on me, because the LORD has anointed me to proclaim good news to the poor."

Twice in Ezekiel we are told that the Spirit of God comes into our lives to give us an undivided heart, and to take away our heart of stone and give us a heart of flesh (36:26–27). What a great prayer: "Lord, take away my heart of stone, and give me a heart of flesh." And, of course, Ezekiel 37 has that great vision of the dry bones. The entire army of Israel is fallen and slain, with nothing but bones left. Can these bones live? The human answer is no. Can any church or denomination in distress, live? The human answer is no. There's no human way. It is only possible through the Spirit of God (Ezek. 37:13–14). In Daniel 5:14, even the pagan king recognizes that Daniel is different. In him is the "spirit of the gods," he says, because he has insight and understanding and wisdom to interpret dreams and have knowledge.

One of the most remarkable passages about the Holy Spirit is found in the second chapter of Joel. This is that wonderful passage that Peter chooses as his text on the day of Pentecost where the Holy Spirit is poured out on all flesh, men and women. The emphasis on the universal gift of the Spirit on all flesh, both men and women, is one of the reasons why we affirm the role of women in ministry. The entire church has been commissioned to proclaim the gospel; we are not going to leave out half the human race. We are all called, through our lives and witness, to proclaim the gospel. We need everybody. Men and women, boys and girls, young and old, high and lowly, all anointed by the Spirit of God.

In Micah 3:8, he says, "I am filled with power, with the Spirit of the LORD." He is saying, in effect, "I can't hold back. I have to proclaim justice. I have to proclaim that Israel has transgressed in their sins." Moving toward the end of the Old Testament we discover that great text in Zechariah, where Zerubbabel doesn't know how he can possibly rebuild the temple and is remembering all the former glories of the good old days, and God says to him, "'Not by might nor by power, but by my Spirit,' says the LORD Almighty" (4:6).

This is just a brief overview of the Old Testament, but I hope it is helping you to see that the Holy Spirit is deeply rooted in every strand of the Old Testament.

Seven Ministries of the Holy Spirit Found in the Old Testament

Another way of thinking about the Holy Spirit in the Old Testament is to examine every mention of the Holy Spirit and try to understand what we can learn about the Spirit. If you study all of the passages together, you will discover that there are seven key ministries of the Holy Spirit found in the Old Testament. Let's explore each one.

First, the Spirit is the source of all life. The source of God's life in us, in you and me, in everybody. This image of God is one of the marks that unites all of humanity. It is the Spirit of God who gives life to us and marks us as bearers of the image of God. Another way of saying this is that it is the Holy Spirit who makes us distinct from the animals. This is why Jesus, in John 20:22, breathed on the disciples and said, "receive the Holy Spirit." It was meant to be a recollection of the first creation, even as Jesus inaugurated the new creation which was now breaking in upon the people of God.

Second, the Spirit is the one who makes God's revelation known to us. We believe that God is a God of self-disclosure. That means that he longs for us to know him and to understand his ways. God has not only revealed his Word to us, but he helps us to understand it and apply it to our lives by his Spirit. This should be a normal part of our Christian experience as we read God's Word, or hear it proclaimed. In fact, Paul makes the Spirit's guidance in our lives one of the defining marks of the Christian when he declares, "those who led by the Spirit of God, are children of God" (Rom. 8:14).

Third, the Spirit grants us discernment and wisdom. We all face many decisions in our lives, as well as the need to understand how to raise our children, or how to respond to various challenges in the surrounding culture. This requires wisdom and discernment. The Holy Spirit gives us the wisdom and discernment when we need it. My wife and I, like many of you, have faced important decisions and major crossroads throughout our life together. As we prayed and asked God for guidance, he has faithfully led us through the power and ministry of the Holy Spirit. We see this in the Jerusalem council where the apostles asked for wisdom when they were responding to God's work among the Gentiles. They preceded their decision by the wonderful phrase, "It seemed good to the Holy Spirit and to us to lay upon you no greater burden than these essentials" (Acts 15:28).

Fourth, the Spirit anoints us for effective service and leadership. The gifts of the Spirit not only include the gift to pastor or teach, but also the gift of administration or leadership or service. All of us have gifts that God has given us to use for his glory. The Spirit helps us to discover our gifts and then he empowers us for the effective use of those gifts.

Fifth, the Spirit convicts of sin and unites our hearts that we might not sin. This ministry of the Holy Spirit begins before we even become Christians, as he brings conviction of our sins and helps us to see our need for Christ. It continues on throughout our Christian lives as he purifies us and makes us holy. The Holy Spirit, for example, is the one who prompts our heart to ask someone to forgive us, or prompts us to pray for someone, or give them a word of encouragement. In the Upper Room teachings of Jesus, he taught us that one of the roles of the Holy Spirit is to "convict the world of guilt in regard to sin and righteousness and judgment" (John 16:8).

Sixth, the Spirit manifests the power of God to heal and transform lives and society. The Spirit is always seeking to introduce God's righteous reign and rule in the midst of a fractured, broken world. This work of the Spirit happens both personally (as when we pray for healing in our bodies) as well as in society, as he seeks to set things right which are not aligned with his kingdom. When someone is sick, we are commanded to call for the elders of the church to pray and "anoint him with oil in the name of the Lord" and the prayer offered in faith will "make the sick person well" (James 5:14–15). Oil, as we shall explore, is one of the symbols of the Holy Spirit in the Bible.

Finally, the Spirit universalizes God's presence to all nations. The Spirit is always beckoning us out into the world to extend God's rule and reign to all peoples, particularly those who have not yet called upon him. It was the Holy Spirit who spoke to the church at Antioch and called Paul and Barnabus into the fruitful, church-planting work that we know today as his three missionary journeys (see Acts 13:1–3).

One thing that is so amazing about God's Word (among many things) is that those seven ministries of the Holy Spirit, which are all taught in the Old Testament, are brought over, celebrated, and renewed in the New Testament. They bud in the Old Testament, and they come into full flowering in the New Testament.

Seven Metaphors of the Spirit in the Old Testament

There are also seven images of the Spirit that are found in the Old Testament. These include the dove, the cloud, fire, the breath/voice of God, the wind, water, and oil. We see the dove at Noah's ark. We see the fire and cloud of God leading his people, and his fire in the burning bush calling forth Moses to lead his people. We see the breath of God at creation, and later, in Ezekiel's vision. We hear the voice of God's Spirit speaking through the prophets, and we see the Spirit's presence in wind, water, and the use of oil in anointing men and women for leadership.

All seven of the metaphors for the Holy Spirit found in the Old Testament find their way into the New Testament, demonstrating the continuity of the Spirit's work between the Old Testament and the New Testament. We meet the dove descending on Jesus at his baptism, a sign of the Holy Spirit. We see fire and wind on the day of Pentecost. We see breath as Jesus breathes on his disciples in John 20:22, imparting the Holy Spirit. Water, of course, is central to baptism, and also as the cleansing work of the Holy Spirit. Oil is used for anointing for the Spirit's power and wisdom in leadership. And the cloud represents the manifest presence of God in the transfiguration of Jesus to the disciples on the holy mountain.

All seven images are brought over. The point is, when we come to the public ministry of Christ being launched, Jesus is being revealed in continuity with the

Old Testament. In Luke 3:21–22, we find three things happening as Jesus is baptized. First, Jesus is baptized in *water*. Then, the heavens are opened up, and the Holy Spirit descends on him like a *dove*. And third, a *voice* from heaven says, "You are my Son, whom I love; with you I am well pleased." Now, the Old Testament was the only Scripture our early brothers and sisters in the faith had. As they are watching this baptism, they immediately recognize three of the signs of the Spirit that are present. First, there is the water of baptism. Then, there is the dove, which is a symbol of God's covenant, going back to Noah and the ark. Doves are regarded throughout the literature of the ancient world as a source of direction. Their cooing could be heard over the waters and they would always fly toward land. And so they were very valuable. They symbolize the direction of God through the Holy Spirit. Finally, there is the voice of Yahweh speaking from heaven, which is the revelation of God.

So, from the very outset when you read the inauguration of Jesus' ministry in Luke, you are seeing that Jesus is being anointed by the Holy Spirit in a way that makes sense to them because of what they know from the Old Testament. The Spirit ties everything together, from creation to Bezalel to judges to kings to the prophets, culminating in Jesus.

Jesus and the Spirit

When we read about the temptation of Jesus in Luke 4, we find that God tests those who receive the Spirit. Jesus is filled with the Holy Spirit, and led by the Holy Spirit out into the wilderness where he will be tested. Then, Luke 4:14 describes what happens to him after the temptations. It does not say that he was *filled* with the Spirit, but that he comes out in the *power* of the Holy Spirit. There's a distinct language difference. After the temptation, he goes into Galilee, in the *power* of the Holy Spirit, to the synagogue in Capernaum, where he opens the scroll of Isaiah, and he reads these opening words of his public ministry:

> "The Spirit of the Lord is on me, because he has anointed me to proclaim good news to the poor. He has sent me to proclaim freedom for the prisoners and recovery of sight for the blind, to set the oppressed free, to proclaim the year of the Lord's favor." (Luke 4:18–19)

As Jesus goes forth into his public ministry, the Spirit of God is present with him to preach, to proclaim, and to heal. He is empowered by the Holy Spirit for his ministry, and we also can be filled and empowered by the Spirit, just as Jesus was. Jesus is showing us how to live our lives fully in the power of the Holy Spirit.

Two

Cracking the Door between Resurrection and Pentecost

Scriptural Background: Acts 1:4–5;
Luke 24:44–49; John 20:19–23

The Gap between the Work of Christ and the Work of the Holy Spirit

Many Christians sense a gap in their knowledge of the person and work of Jesus and the person and work of the Holy Spirit. We all need help to deepen our own experience with the Holy Spirit. There are three broad channels through which the Holy Spirit acts in our lives. First, he empowers us to exercise our gifts and to enable us to bring the gospel of Jesus Christ to the world. This is God's power for a global mission. Second, he purifies us and makes us to be more holy like Christ. This is God's work in sanctifying us and conforming us to the likeness of Christ. Finally, it is the Holy Spirit who gives us wisdom and discernment. This is needed for our guidance as well as our having a biblical, godly perspective on various challenges we face each day.

The basic problem in the church is that we have developed a weak link between the completed work of Christ, with his death and resurrection, and the ongoing work and ministry of the Holy Spirit in the life of the church. If the incarnation is the knot that ties heaven to earth, then Pentecost is surely the knot that ties the church to its holy, empowered mission in the world. Unfortunately, the way we tend to deal with the doctrine of the Holy Spirit in the church today is a persistent benign neglect. Part of the First Great Awakening (1725–1745), including the revivals associated with the Wesleys, was a revisitation of this doctrine, and an intentional effort to understand grace and salvation in a more fully Trinitarian way.

In the previous chapter, we saw how the Holy Spirit was present and active in the Old Testament. We also explored how the Holy Spirit manifested himself in the life of Jesus. This chapter focuses on three passages in the New Testament that give us some snapshots of the post-resurrection, but pre-Pentecost period in the teachings of Christ. Jesus is breaking down this wall that we have erected. He is cracking open the door that we so often have closed. There are three passages which really bring this out found in Acts 1, Luke 24, and John 20.

Acts 1:4–5

In Acts 1:4–5, Jesus says something which is quite surprising. Jesus stands before his disciples as the risen Lord, and he is preparing them (and us) for his departure to heaven. We expect him to say something like, "Okay, troops, go, go, go." He does tell us to go into the world just before his ascension to heaven in Acts 1:7–8. But that is not what he says here. Instead, he first says, "Do not leave Jerusalem." This is very different from the earlier Great Commission passages in the Gospels (like Matthew 28:18–20 and Mark 16:15–16) where he tells us to go into all the world and make disciples and preach the gospel. Instead, here he says, "Do not leave Jerusalem, but wait for the gift my Father promised." This is not a command to "go," but a command to "wait." Why would Jesus tell us to wait before he tells us to go?

Some of us find waiting very difficult. My idea of waiting is like waiting for a light to turn green. But in the Spirit-endowed aspect of my life where God meets me, there have been times when God has brought me into deep waiting, learning to wait for him to prepare me for what he has for me to do or to say. And that waiting is so important. I think that God has given us both the wait and go commands because both are important. The "go" command keeps us from being too passive, which can be a problem; but the "wait" command keeps us from thinking that we can serve him through our own strength and resources.

We need to wait on God and become empowered for service, but often we haven't been taught to do this. Sometimes, it is harder to wait for the disruptive empowerment of the Spirit in the unknown tomorrow than to work in the flesh that we know today. Sometimes it is easier for us to work with the strength from below than to wait for the power from on high. This is why Jesus says, "Wait for the gift my Father promised."

Notice the Trinitarian structure of the passage. Here is the second person of the Trinity instructing us to wait for the gift of the third person of the Trinity, that was promised by the first person of the Trinity. This is an early reminder to us that we need the full ministry of every person of the Trinity in our lives. In verse 4 Jesus says, "Wait for the gift my Father promised, *which you have heard me speak about*" (emphasis added).

In other words, Jesus had already taught them about the Holy Spirit. This is probably a reference to the extended teaching on the Holy Spirit found in John's gospel known as the Upper Room Discourse. It is the final teaching of Christ to his disciples before he goes to the cross. It is found in John 14–17. For example, Jesus says in John 14:16–17, "I will ask the Father, and he will give you another Helper, to be with you forever, even the Spirit of truth" (ESV). Then he said, "These things I have spoken to you while I am still with you. But the Helper, the Holy Spirit, whom the Father will send in my name, he will teach you all things and bring to your remembrance all that I have said to you" (vv. 25–26 ESV).

John 16:7–8 says, "But very truly I tell you, it is for your good that I am going away. Unless I go away, the Advocate will not come to you; but if I go, I will send him to you. When he comes, he will prove the world to be in the wrong about sin and righteousness and judgment."

John 16:13 says, "When he, the Spirit of Truth, comes, he will guide you into all truth. He will not speak on his own [authority]; he will speak only what he hears, and he will tell you what is yet to come."

Now, look at the ministries of the Spirit in these passages. He's going to help us. He's going to teach us.

He's going to bring to remembrance things that Christ has taught. He's going to help us bear witness to him. He's going to convict the world regarding sin. He's going to lead us and guide us into truth and declare what is to come. These texts were very important to the early Christians. They preached *both* the work of Christ *and* the work of the Holy Spirit. Yet, somewhere along the way, the church has forgotten and lost half of the gospel. Today, it seems a lot of us are more "Bi-nitarian" than "Trinitarian." We have to re-embrace the full gospel.

That's why the motto of Asbury Seminary is, "*The Whole Bible for the Whole World.*" What H. C. Morrison meant by that statement was the *whole* gospel, not half the gospel. He was reminding us all to embrace the whole Trinitarian gospel. Jesus is seeking to bridge the gap between his work and the ministry of the Holy Spirit. That is the purpose of this passage.

When we get to Acts 1:5, Jesus says, "John baptized with water, but in a few days, you will be baptized with the Holy Spirit." Now, this is recalling the promise of John the Baptist who prepared the way for the coming of Christ. John had promised that Jesus would baptize us with his Spirit. But this did not happen during the earthly ministry of Jesus. It would not happen until after the resurrection, when he breathed on the disciples and said, "Receive the Holy Spirit" (John 20:22). It also happened repeatedly in the book of Acts from Pentecost onward, and it keeps on happening through the present.

The polytheism concept is hard for Jews + Muslims to accept.

Luke 24:44–49

Remember, Jesus is trying to break down this barrier between his ministry and the ministry of the Holy Spirit. Let's look at Luke 24:46–47. This is also a post-resurrection scene of Christ, and Jesus gives an amazing summary of what we call the gospel narrative: "The Messiah will suffer and rise from the dead on the third day, and repentance for the forgiveness of sins will be preached in his name to all nations, beginning at Jerusalem." This is a significant gospel summary and the only one that appears in the post-resurrection scenes with Christ. But he doesn't stop there. He goes on and says, "I am going to send you what my Father has promised; but stay in the city until you have been clothed with power from on high" (v. 49).

Jesus is talking about an experience that every believer in Christ needs to have, which is known by various expressions such as being "filled with the Holy Spirit," or being "baptized in the Holy Spirit," or, as here, being "clothed

Just breathe & not worry about the process.

25

with power from on high." Power for mission. Power for holiness. We are to wait for this power that God has planned for us to have as the people of God.

John 20:19–23

Finally, we come to the John 20 passage on the evening of Easter. In John's version of the Great Commission, Jesus says, "Peace be with you! As the Father has sent me, I am sending you" (v. 21). But then the passage goes on to say that he breathed on them and said, "Receive the Holy Spirit" (v. 22). Here you have the breath of Jesus on the disciples imparting the Holy Spirit before the day of Pentecost arrives.

So, what is happening here? There are four things I want to highlight. First, this is the breath of the new creation. There is no Jew on the planet that would have heard this and not immediately thought of Genesis 2:7. In Genesis 2:7, God forms the man and woman, and he breathes into them the Holy Spirit. He breathes the *ruah* of God, the Spirit of God, into us and makes us living beings. That is the creational act. Here, he breathes again. This time, it is the breath of the new creation. This is almost like a second creation account, but now it is the *new* creation—this is what it means to be endowed with the Spirit to usher in the new reality of God's kingdom, his rule and reign in the world and in our lives.

Second, this reinforces that Jesus is the Baptizer of the Holy Spirit. John had said in Luke 3:16, "I baptize you with water. But one who is more powerful than I will come . . . He will baptize you with the Holy Spirit and fire." So again, there is no closed doorway between Jesus' ministry and the Holy Spirit because Jesus *is* the Baptizer. And, by the way, this door that we have erected gets opened from both directions. On the one hand, Jesus is the one that opens the door. He not only cracks it open, but he kicks it open. He is the one who makes sure that through the Spirit you are being made holy, that you have discernment, and that you are empowered for mission.

But the Holy Spirit also opens the door from the other direction as well. He won't let you forget that you could not come to Christ without his ministry and conviction, and he is the one who brings back to our minds all that Christ said and did. The Holy Spirit is the one who convicts the world regarding sin. The Holy Spirit is active even in unbelievers, convicting of sin and drawing them to Christ. No one comes to Christ unless the Father draws him (John 6:44), and he draws us through the power of the Spirit. So we have the Spirit's work in prevenient grace (grace that comes before we are justified), preparing us to receive God's grace. We cannot be justified without the Holy Spirit's work. He is active in bringing us to Christ. He is active as we abide in Christ. He is always active. But the point is that we need *more* of the Holy Spirit in our lives.

Third, this text teaches us that Pentecost is not merely a singular event. The Spirit of God *keeps* falling down. The Spirit of God comes in John 20, but again in Acts 2, and then in Acts 4, 6, 7, 8, 9, 10, 13, and 19. Are you seeing a pattern here? It happens a lot. Once we go through all of these texts, and further subsequent texts in the Epistles, we find that there are eight different expressions used for the Holy Spirit coming into our lives. We love to choose one, and want everybody to use that same language. But the New Testament doesn't do that. We have already seen that "clothed with power" is used in Luke 24. But other expressions are also used. The phrase, "baptized with the Holy Spirit" occurs twice. "Receiving the Holy Spirit" appears eight times. The Holy Spirit "coming upon" or "falling upon" appears four times. Three times we are told that the Holy Spirit was "poured out." The most common expression is the phrase, "being filled with the Holy Spirit," which appears eight times. Finally, four times we are told that the Spirit has been "given to us." It doesn't really matter what you call it, just make sure that you get it! God still wants to keep on pouring out his Spirit upon us. Keep getting filled with the Spirit. Be baptized with the Holy Spirit. Be sanctified by the ongoing presence and power of the Holy Spirit in your life.

Fourth, the language of *receive* is related here to the third person of the Trinity. Now, this is one of the great things about this passage. Jesus breathes on them and he says, "Receive the Holy Spirit." We have a mountain of evangelistic literature that asks people to receive Jesus Christ, which is wonderful. It is almost iconic in the Christian world to hear someone say, "I have received Jesus Christ as my Lord and Savior." That has become a classic phrase. But we have no comparable emphasis on receiving the Holy Spirit. When was the last time you heard someone say, "I have received the Holy Spirit as my personal Sanctifier"? But, in the New Testament, it is just as important for someone to say, "I have received the Holy Spirit," as it is to say, "I have received Jesus Christ." As I noted in chapter 1, God is not merely interested in forgiving us, he also wants to transform us. That is what all of this is about. We must get away from the low-bar

Christianity which says, "What is the *least* one has to do to become a Christian?" That is minimalistic Christianity. We need a fresh dose of New Testament Christianity. We want to know what is the *most* God can do in our life, not what is the least we must do to get us through to heaven. God is not just providing "fire insurance." He is in the business of transforming the whole of our lives, both now and in the life to come!

God's power transforms lives. Abraham leaves his family, becomes a homeless wanderer and a father of a nation. Joseph is sold into slavery and rescues a people. Moses flees to Midian, stands in the presence of a burning bush, and becomes a deliverer. Naomi and Ruth return to their home empty, but discover the providence of God. Gideon stands fearful in the winepress and is called to lead an army. David is tending sheep and suddenly finds himself slaying a giant and being promised a throne. Jonah is scared and running away from God, and he ends up preaching the gospel to the Ninevites. The widow of Nain is on her way to the cemetery and ends up with a resurrection party. Zacchaeus climbs a tree and finds divine acceptance. A bunch of fishermen are mending nets and end up embarking on a mission to the nations of the whole world.

What is the theme in all of this? That God is taking ordinary people like you and me, and by his Spirit, he is transforming us to be a part of his mission in the world. Can we say amen to that? We need more than a tepid, easy-to-swallow, so-called gospel that is void of power, holiness, and transformation. We want a rebirth of New Testament Christianity. We want that holy desperation for more of God, which is the only soil that God uses to bring forth renewal and awakening in the church.

Three

The Church Is on Fire!

Scriptural Background: Acts 2:1–13

Leonard Ravenhill once said, "There is no greater tragedy than a sick church in a dying world." Is there something in you that is just desperately longing for the rebirth of a real church on mission to a world hungry for the gospel of Jesus Christ? We can have no mission to the world until we, as the people of God, rediscover the gospel ourselves. That is the story of the Reformation in the sixteenth century. It is the story of the Pietistic movement in the seventeenth century. It is the story of the Wesleyan Revivals and the First Great Awakening (1725–1745) in the eighteenth century. It is the story of the Second Great Awakening (1790–1840) and the birth of the modern missions movement in the nineteenth century. It is the story of the Pentecostal revivals of the twentieth century. All of these movements began by the gospel first being rediscovered by people who already called themselves Christians.

The Prophecy of Joel

In times like this, we can find hope in the prophecy of Joel, who captured what it was like to live in a time of ecclesial exile, where all you have is a desperation and a hope that God might act and breathe new life into the people of God. Jeremiah, Ezekiel, Habakkuk, Joel, Ezra, and Nehemiah are your lifeblood. These are great wells to draw upon as a church, to help us negotiate safe passage through our time. I did a little survey of Joel to see all the people that he has called to repentance. I have a partial list here to make the point: old people, young people, men, women, children, drunkards, farmers, servants, priests, Jews, non-Jews, nations under covenant, nations not under covenant. He covers the whole field. Everyone is going in one direction, and Joel is saying, "No, you are going the wrong way. Yahweh is this way. The covenant is this way. Salvation is this way." In the midst of all of this, the nation is being completely destroyed. But Joel lifts up his eyes and he catches this vision.

He says, "And it shall come to pass afterward, that I will pour out my Spirit on all flesh; your sons and your daughters shall prophesy, your old men shall dream dreams, and your young men shall see visions. Even on the male and female servants in those days I will pour out my Spirit" (Joel 2:28–29 ESV). Don't you love that? Here is Joel, in an ecclesial disaster, and he captures the great reversal. He discovers that God's plan is still intact.

Jeremiah is on the brink of horrible disaster. The Babylonians are taking over the country. He has seen the humiliation and the dismantlement of the nation. Jews are being locked in chains and put on carts to Babylon. Others, in disobedience, are fleeing back to Egypt. What does Jeremiah do? He buys a piece of land. If we were being completely taken over, everything destroyed, the last thing you would do is buy a piece of land. He buys the field of Anathoth from his cousin Hanamel. He weighs out seventeen shekels of silver, takes a deed, and gives it to Baruch. Jeremiah 32:15 says, "For this is what the LORD Almighty, the God of Israel, says: 'Houses, fields and vineyards will again be bought in this land.'"

Now that's a vision. That's what I call an exilic purchase. He buys the field at Anathoth because he is caught up in a greater narrative. He was tuned into a narrative that was louder than the deafening march of the Babylonian armies. And that's not easy. Can you hear the footsteps of Jesus in the midst of the clamoring boots of this culture? Jeremiah, likewise, looked up, and he saw the covenant. In Jeremiah 31:33–34, the Lord says, "I will put my law in their minds and write [a new covenant] on their hearts. . . . No longer will they teach their neighbor, or say to one another, 'Know the LORD,' because they will all know me, from the least of them to the greatest."

Jeremiah caught a vision of a better day. John the Baptist, at the end of four hundred years of waiting on all kinds of promises, mostly unfulfilled, also looked up and said, "I baptize with water, but one who is coming after me will baptize with the Holy Spirit and with fire" (see Matthew 3:11). You see, they are all pointing to a day when God would come and do something that we cannot do on our own, something that only the triune God can do.

The Day of Pentecost

Acts chapter 2 opens with the words, "When the day of Pentecost arrived . . ." (ESV). The word *Pentecost* is used because it means fiftieth. After the Passover and the Exodus, the Israelites traveled fifty days before they got to Mount Sinai where God gave them his Law and entered into a covenant with them. The feast which celebrates the giving of the Law became known as Pentecost, because the Law was given fifty days after the Passover.

It is no mistake that Jesus was crucified at the time of Passover. It is all part of the reenactment of God's redemptive themes. Christ is the sacrificial Lamb, just like the lamb on Passover. And after forty days of appearing to many, Christ ascends to the Father, and tells his disciples to wait. Then there are ten days of waiting. God is actually waiting for the right moment in the redemptive calendar. If you ever had any doubt that God loves the liturgical calendar, here it is. Even God waits for ten days, because the Spirit's coming needs to happen on Pentecost. Pentecost was the day when God gave the Law on Mount Sinai. So on *this* Pentecost, God will write his law on our hearts through the Holy Spirit.

I've often thought of that ten-day wait in terms of the redemption calendar. But I wonder, what are the disciples thinking? What are they doing? Are they shooting pool? Watching YouTube videos? Playing some kind of video game? What are they doing? Drinking coffee?

They are in desperation. They do not know what to do. God has broken into their lives in this amazing reality of the resurrection. Christ has appeared to them, but they are still behind locked doors, trying to figure out what is happening. They are praying and fasting. They are realizing that whatever is going to happen will be messy, disruptive, and will change their lives forever.

You may have thought that Christian discipleship was about education and inspiration alone. Perhaps you hear inspiring sermons on Sunday, or you attend a great Sunday school class. But God wants to do more than inspire you, or even educate you. He wants to transform you. Your whole life must be transformed by the power of the Spirit. God has a plan for us and for our lives, and he won't accept something halfway. When you look for the fire of God to fall upon your life, be ready. Getting filled with the Holy Spirit will change your life and your church forever, because you can't receive the Spirit of God until you are at the end of your rope. Amazingly, God will not fill you until he first empties you.

If you are feeling empty today, it might be the very place you need to be. You can't build a fire that he alone can light. You can't blow a wind that he alone can blow. And no class or seminar or inspiring sermon can get you to that place. And so, Acts 2 is really about divine disruption. Let's look at three disruptions that appear in the text.

Three Divine Disruptions

The first one is found in verse 2: *the blowing of a mighty wind of God.* Now when Jews read this Scripture about the breath, or wind, of God, as we pointed out in chapter 2, they thought about that first breath of Eden that breathed God's life and image into us. It separates us from the animals. But this is the second breath of the new creation. This separates us from all the human-driven initiatives, and allows us to be fully empowered by the Spirit to walk with God in his mission in the world. This breath is actually a mighty wind that will blow away all of our comfortable Christianity.

The second disruption happens in verse 3: *the fire of God falls.* The Jews interpreted fire as purification and guidance. They couldn't help but remember the fire that fell on Elijah's sacrifice. It demonstrates God's power over all human constructs and all the altars we would build. They also remembered the fire in the wilderness that guided them in their greatest need in the darkness—that pillar of fire by night. So this fire purifies, it purges, and it guides—all things that God does in us when the Spirit comes into our lives.

We rightfully celebrate the incarnation—Jesus Christ, stepping into human flesh. But Pentecost is about the third person of the Trinity stepping into human flesh—into our lives, our bodies, our experiences. In chapter 1, we identified seven metaphors in the Old Testament that point to the Holy Spirit (the dove, the cloud, fire, the breath/voice of God, the wind, water, and oil), and we looked at how these reappeared in the New Testament. We already encountered the water and dove at Christ's baptism. In the upper room, we saw the breath, as Jesus breathed onto disciples to receive the Holy Spirit. Here, in Acts 2, we find two more of them: wind and fire. The fire of God is absolutely crucial. It is the power and guidance of the Spirit coming upon the church. We should "not leave home without it."

The third disruption is *speaking in tongues*. In verse 4, we are told that they actually spoke in other tongues as the Spirit enabled them. Let me say up front, whether you personally do or do not speak in tongues is not really as important as some have made it out to be. The book of Acts highlights a wide range of ways in which people bear witness to the Spirit. Speaking in tongues is simply one of them. I believe it is fully operative today, as the book of Corinthians tells us, but Paul says that not all speak in tongues. The point that he makes in Corinthians is clear: the purpose of tongue-speaking, as with all the gifts, is to edify the body (see 1 Corinthians 12). So the question is, how does this experience edify the body? When you read the text, you see that each one heard about the mighty acts of God in their own languages—Parthians; Medes; Elamites; residents of Mesopotamia, Judea, Cappadocia, Pontus and Asia, Phrygia and Pamphylia, Egypt, parts of Libya near the Cyrene; visitors from Rome; Cretans and Arabs.

The wondrous acts of God were being declared in all the languages of the people who had gathered. What does this mean? That's the crucial question. What would this mean to the people who were there? How would they understand this? God was doing something that they would understand in a certain way. Look back to Genesis 11, and think about the amazing experience at the Tower of Babel, when all the languages were divided and scattered. Here, at Pentecost, that all gets reversed, and the world's languages are united again.

Pentecost also looks to the future. The day of Pentecost not only reverses the curse of the past, but it also looks forward to the new creation. You can't read this experience of Acts 2 without realizing that it anticipates that day when a multitude that no one can count, from every tribe and nation and people and language, stands before the throne and before the Lamb (Rev. 7:9). That is God's global vision. The church is, in fact, the most ethnically diverse movement in the history of the world. We are currently living into all the realities of that final day. The speaking in tongues is simply a foreshadowing of that great day at the climax of the ages.

On the day of Pentecost, we encounter one of three great streams of the Holy Spirit in the life of the church—power for global witness. The other two are holiness and sanctified purity in our lives, and discernment/wisdom for life's challenges. The first, which we see in this text, is the power for a global witness. Over the years, I've heard many slogans about Asbury, but I think that the most persistent slogan is, "The place where head and heart go hand in hand." It is a good phrase, and it highlights the importance of connecting our thinking with our heart. But the work of the Holy Spirit applies to the head, heart, *and* to our actions. Perhaps we should say, "Where head and heart go hand in hand, so that the feet can run!"

When the tongue-speaking at Pentecost happens, it is a sign of the global witness of the church. Whenever a church experiences renewal and awakening, the purpose is not simply to solve our problems. Renewal actually thrusts us out to the ends of the earth. It gives us a burden for the lost—those who have never heard the gospel, whether it be a millennial who has just lost the memory of the gospel, or some people group that has never heard the gospel. There are thousands of groups of people that do not have even so much as John 3:16 in their language. In India, where I've worked, there are 2,000 people groups with no Christian witness. China has 444, Russia has 117, and on and on it goes. Who will purchase those fields? Will any of you say, "Lord, I'm going to purchase one of those fields for the gospel"? Who will speak those languages? We need people to go to the ends of the earth. For some of you, the "end of the earth" may be right where you are in your own town or city. But we should always be lifting up our eyes to see the harvest that is around us.

We have been in survival mode way too long. We have been preoccupied with our inner angst way too long. There is a great global vision that has been poured out for us. I hope that this book helps to get you out of survival mode, out of your comfort zone, and going to a place that's disruptive. Just be willing to say, "Lord, take me to a place that's not easy for me, but where your disruptive power will flow in me and through me."

That could be a hundred different places for a hundred people. There is no one set way or place. One person's disruption is another person's easy place, but each one of us has to be willing for God to put us in places where we experience disruption so that we can incorporate more of the power of the Holy Spirit in our lives. And the great thing about that disruption, is that in the long run, we end up realizing that we have become more fully alive.

We all need to be filled with the Holy Spirit. We all need to capture a vision for the new creation that is even now breaking into the present day. In this world, if there is any message that we are sensing right now in our society, it is that this world is broken. There is no political solution to our problems. There is no legal solution. Congress can't fix it. This is a deeply spiritual problem, and the only answer is the preaching of the gospel. That will only happen when we rediscover the gospel and the fire of the Holy Spirit, who will send us to those hard places where we can become a part of what God is doing in the world.

Four

Pentecost Revisited: Power for Bold Preaching

Scriptural Background: Acts 3 and 4

D. L. Moody, the great nineteenth-century evangelist, was once asked how he could possibly open the Bible, whether to Nehemiah, the Psalms, or Leviticus, and end up with an altar call to receive Christ. He responded that it didn't matter where he started, because he always made a beeline to the gospel.

You might expect that, coming from a full-time evangelist like D. L. Moody, but maybe there is something here that we should take notice of. When you read the sermons throughout the book of Acts, the apostles start at many different places. They may start from the Law, the Prophets, or the writings, but they always end at the gospel. They always bring it to the centrality of Jesus Christ, crucified and risen. In the light of the empty tomb, they see Jesus everywhere. Jesus is the Suffering Servant of Isaiah. Jesus is the rock out of which water came in the wilderness. Jesus is the stone the builders rejected that has become the Cornerstone. Jesus becomes the archetype of the priest Melchizedek. Jesus is the seed of the woman who crushes the serpent's head. Jesus is Lord, under whose feet all nations will be placed. He seems to fill the whole frame—law, priest, king, and sacrifice. Jesus is the subject of every sermon, the fulfillment of every promise, and the hope of all the ages.

The Nature of Apostolic Preaching

We know that this God-ordained, Spirit-empowered, Christo-centric preaching is the source of the boldness of the apostolic message. If you actually take time to look at all of the sermons in the New Testament, you find that the apostles do not preach like we do today. It doesn't happen. You never hear about some clever idea. They never offer a self-help technique. Their sermons seldom even offer a moralistic admonition like we find in the epistles of Paul,

Peter, or John. Yet, this is what dominates most preaching today. In contrast, the New Testament preaches a person. They preach Jesus Christ.

One of the themes of this book is to explore the three great channels through which the Holy Spirit works in our lives: power for global witness, holiness for sanctified purity, and discernment for faithful living. Acts 3 and 4 give a detailed account of that first theme extended—the empowered witness of the church. Peter and John are entering the temple, and they see a beggar who had been lame since birth. The beggar asks for money, but the apostles say, "Silver or gold I do not have, but what I do have I give you. In the name of Jesus Christ of Nazareth, walk" (Acts 3:6). The man is healed; he enters the temple, walking and leaping. The ministry of Jesus is unfolding in the life of the apostles. The good news is that we can be doing the works of Jesus, and miracles can unfold through the church the way they unfolded through Jesus. We have the joy of people being healed, but also the opposition with the authorities, as happened with Jesus. When we become like Jesus, we have to take on the whole package.

Peter had proclaimed the centrality of Christ on the day of Pentecost, and three thousand responded. When the gospel was boldly preached, the people responded. In this particular passage, they again preach the gospel, but before they can have the altar call, they are arrested and taken away to the authorities. Even with that, two thousand more people responded. Now that is amazing!

Something is happening. This is disruptive. The authorities want to know by what power or name the apostles do these things. Their question is answered by the name that is at the root of the apostles' authority. They are not promoting webinars or self-help techniques. They say it is the name of Jesus that is the power of their preaching and of their healing. This is not a conflict with the secular unbelieving culture, but with the religious authorities. The apostles were not ordained priests. They had no official sanction. They weren't seminary graduates. They didn't have any letters behind their names or titles in front of their names. All they had was the name of Jesus.

Now we come to the third sermon in Acts. It is preaching that is again filled with boldness and courage (Acts 4:13). Notice in Acts 4:8, after the question about where they got their power, Peter, "filled with the Holy Spirit," replied. Peter had been in the upper room when Jesus breathed on the disciples and said, "Be filled with the Holy Spirit." He was there on the day of Pentecost when *everyone* was filled with the Holy Spirit in a dramatic fashion. Wasn't he already filled with the Holy Spirit? Yet, here is Peter being filled with the Spirit again. Twice in this chapter alone we find that Peter is again filled with the Holy Spirit.

What does that teach us? It teaches us that the day of Pentecost is not a singular event in the same way as the cross, resurrection, and ascension are singular events. Pentecost is meant to be one of those never-ending days. Pentecost continues to unfold in the life of the church and the ministry of the Holy Spirit. In Acts 4:31, we find that Peter is filled with the Holy Spirit a fourth time in order to "[speak] the word of God boldly." Remember that in Ephesians 5:18, Paul tells us not to be drunk with wine, but to be filled with the Holy Spirit. He is saying that the Holy Spirit is better than drinking wine. It literally means do not continually get drunk, but continually be filled with the Holy Spirit. The word in the original language is *hyruthsay*, which is a present, continuous imperative. It is also in the passive voice—you are *being* filled. It isn't something you manufacture. God fills us with the Holy Spirit. That means that when we are filled with the Holy Spirit, God is the one who turns the faucet on.

Personal Testimony

In my own life I had a very profound, life-changing encounter with the Holy Spirit in September of 1977. I'll never forget the experience. I was filled to the brim and overflowing with the Holy Spirit. It was every bit as powerful as Jesus breathing on me and saying, "Receive the Holy Spirit," or being there in the upper room when the tongues of fire came down. And if you had said to me weeks or months after that event, "Are you filled with the Holy Spirit?" I would have replied, "Yes!" I thought that once the fire of God fell, once the wind blew into my life, I would never again feel dry as toast in my spirit. But I soon realized what most of us already know: we leak. We need refills. That's why Paul says to keep on being filled with the Holy Spirit.

Power for Bold Preaching

Sometimes those of us with seminary degrees preach only out of our training. I've done this too. We know how to do good work for Jesus by preaching and teaching, but there's something missing. As important as it is to preach, it is not enough if you are not also filled and empowered by the Holy Spirit. We must have that unction because it is always a divine event, not just a human event, when we preach the gospel or live our lives for Christ. Maybe you have only the Christianity you were taught as a child in Sunday school, and you are finding it inadequate for what you are facing as an adult. Perhaps it time to go to a new level in your relationship with Jesus Christ.

In Acts 4:8, Peter is filled with the Holy Spirit and he proclaims that it is in the name of Jesus Christ of Nazareth that this formerly crippled man stands completely healthy. And then Peter quotes Psalm 118 about Jesus being the stone that the builders rejected which has now become the chief cornerstone. Peter, through divine, spiritual insight, understands that Psalm 118 is really a prophecy about Jesus Christ the Cornerstone. That happens through the infilling of the Holy Spirit. That is when he also says, "Salvation is found in no one else, for there is no other name under heaven given to mankind by which we must be saved" (Acts 4:12).

That is the gospel in seed form. When the leaders see the apostles' boldness despite being uneducated, common men, they are astonished. They go from being annoyed or perplexed to being amazed. These men don't have degrees. They don't have training, but they are speaking with power and courage and boldness. God is doing something in them and through them, and the leaders are astonished.

In stark contrast, I doubt many people are astonished today when they witness the life of the church. They're often bored. One of the things that is missing is the unction of the Holy Spirit, the power that infuses whatever gifts we offer. In Acts 4:19–20, we see an example of the wisdom of the Holy Spirit. The leaders admonish the apostles not to speak or teach any more in the name of Jesus. Peter replies that whether it is right in the sight of God to listen to others rather than to God, they must judge, but that he cannot help but speak of what they have seen and heard.

It is a bold statement, but it is also laced with wisdom. It shows respect for the authorities, but also says that they are not going to stop their witness. They are going to appeal to a higher court and let God attest whether what they are saying is true. We see not only the disruptive power for global witness, but also now the discerning wisdom for faithful living.

That is amazing! That is why Jesus said, "When you are brought before synagogues, rulers and authorities, do not worry about how you will defend yourselves or what you will say, for the Holy Spirit will teach you at that time what you should say" (Luke 12:11–12). This is not even remotely denying the importance of good training; it is reminding us that in addition to good training, we also need the Holy Spirit to teach us and to have bold power when preaching the Word of God.

The apostles are released from custody. They return to their friends and a huge worship service breaks out. They again quote the Psalms, "Why do the nations rage and the peoples plot in vain? The kings of the earth set themselves, and the rulers take counsel together, against the Lord and against his Anointed" (2:1–2 ESV). Then they make the application to Jesus. Jesus is the anointed one against whom the kings of the earth are taking their stand. The apostles pray and ask the Lord to continue to help them to speak the Word of God with all boldness. Then the Holy Spirit comes on them and the place is shaken. It's like another day of Pentecost. The place is shaken just like we saw in Acts 2. They are again filled with the Holy Spirit. This is the fourth time Peter is filled with the Holy Spirit.

They continue to speak the Word of God with boldness. There it is again. The boldness of preaching is tied to the infilling of the Holy Spirit and the ability to proclaim God's Word with the centrality of Jesus Christ. That is what marks all of the apostles' preaching. Perhaps you are now getting an insight into what the church needs today. The modern church has domesticated the gospel and has watered it down by turning church into a human-driven enterprise. We have lost our focus on the work of the Holy Spirit. That may not be your experience at church, but it is the experience of many. We need a recovery of biblical Christianity and Spirit-empowered preaching.

Locking Preachers in the Pulpit!

Stanley Hauerwas, the well-known Methodist ethicist and theologian from Duke Divinity School, shared an interesting story from an experience he had in Edinburgh. Edinburgh is a beautiful city with many amazing churches with interesting features, such as raised pulpits and long stairways ascending to the pulpit. My wife and I had the privilege of living in Edinburgh for three years while I was doing doctoral studies.

Hauerwas was giving the Gifford Lectures, a famous lectureship in Edinburgh, and asked to preach at St. Mary's Cathedral in Edinburgh. One of the practices at St. Mary's since the Reformation is that the sexton leads the preacher to the pulpit, opens the pulpit door for the preacher, and then closes the door, locking it. Stanley Hauerwas said it was a very interesting feeling to be locked into the pulpit—and he found out that they won't let you out of the pulpit until you preach the gospel! Now I'm not advocating that we lock our preachers in the pulpit, but I love the instinct. Go into the pulpit and preach the gospel! Don't leave until you do. Make a beeline to the gospel.

That is what D. L. Moody taught us. If you are reading about Adam in the garden, remember that Christ is the second Adam (see Romans 5). If you are reading about the manna in the wilderness, you should remember that Jesus is the true manna from heaven (John 6). If you are reading about Jonah in the belly of the fish, it would be helpful to remember that the Gospels teach that just as Jonah was in the belly of the fish for three days, Christ was in the belly of the earth for three days. And just as Jonah came out of that fish to preach the gospel to the nations, so Jesus came out of the empty tomb to preach the gospel to the nations. Read the Psalms, and begin to see Jesus in every psalm! My wife and I get up early every morning and sing a metrical psalm. The more time we spend in the Psalms, the more we find Jesus there. D. L. Moody was right. All Scripture points to Jesus. That is one of the gifts which the Spirit gives us as we read Scripture.

This is the message of Acts 3 and 4. We are learning something about the preaching of the apostles. We should be praying for bolder preaching in the pulpits of our country. The pulpit has become a dry and weary place, void of the power and anointing of God. If we are going to see an awakening in our culture, it must begin with us. We have spent so much of our time trying to make the church look and feel like the surrounding popular culture, we have forgotten that the church has been called to be shockingly distinctive from anything in the world. The Spirit longs to do a new work in the church. It begins with you and me being filled with the Spirit, and receiving the boldness to witness for him in all that we do.

Five

Receiving the Spirit: Crisis Event or Ongoing Process?

Scriptural Background: Acts 8:1–11:19

Do you remember the last words of Jesus, in his public ministry on earth, found in Holy Scripture? They are not found in the Gospels. They are found in the book of Acts, just prior to the ascension of Christ. He said to us, the church of all ages, "You will receive power when the Holy Spirit comes on you; and you will be my witnesses in Jerusalem, and in all Judaea and Samaria, and to the ends of the earth" (Acts 1:8).

It's a remarkable way to end one's ministry, right? Think about it. This great promise that we will be filled with the Spirit. This amazing call that we are going to reach the ends of the earth. It is almost a restatement of that messianic prophecy of Jesus in Isaiah 49:6 which says, "I will make you as a light for the nations, that my salvation may reach to the ends of the earth" (ESV).

Luke uses Acts 1:8, the final Great Commission, to give us the framework for the book of Acts—the order of Jerusalem, Judaea, Samaria, and the ends of the earth. We may think of this in terms of what I call the 24,901-mile mandate. If you take the earth's circumference at its largest point and go around the world at its circumference, it's 24,901 miles. Think of Jerusalem, Judaea, Samaria, and the ends of the earth in terms of geographic expansion. The church is going to start out in Jerusalem and eventually travel the 24,901 miles around the world, symbolically speaking. But there is a lot more going on than that. It is also about an *ethnic* progression that brings the gospel from Jewish people who come to know Jesus Christ as the Messiah, filling Jewish hopes and expectations; to Samaritans, a different group who were mixed-Jewish people; and then, eventually, to the ends of the earth where the Gentiles throughout the world see Jesus Christ as the Lord for all nations. That is what is beginning here.

We are going to look at this remarkable transition part of Acts, from 8:1 to 11:19, where the gospel is brought from Samaria to the ends of the earth. You can almost feel Luke's energy here. He is so excited to get us to that point when the gospel in Acts 11:23 is preached to Gentiles, but there is a lot that has to happen in the transitional part of Acts first. Philip goes to Samaria and experiences a revival. He meets the Ethiopian eunuch on the desert road, Cornelius's household is converted, and Saul has his dramatic experience on the road to Damascus. It is a remarkable part of Acts. There is a lot of anticipation in Acts to get us to the point where the gospel spills out into the Gentile world. The text begins in Acts 8:1, "On that day a great persecution broke out against the church in Jerusalem, and all except the apostles were scattered throughout Judea and Samaria."

Persecution pushes the church out into Samaria. We are told in the text that the apostles remain in Jerusalem. I used to chide the apostles for this, but I don't see it that way anymore. I really see the apostles strategically staying in Jerusalem as the more difficult thing to do, anticipating the ingathering of thousands of Jews to Christ, which was also happening at this same time. We saw in Acts 2 that three thousand were saved. In Acts 4, two thousand more come forward. In Acts 6:7, Luke says that a great number of priests were coming to the Lord. From the apostles' perspective, they are seeing a huge ingathering of Israel, and they can't help but think that Isaiah 60:3 (ESV), "Nations shall come to your light, and kings to the brightness of your rising," is being fulfilled before their eyes.

Diaspora 2.0

In verses 1 and 4 of Acts 8 we see the word "scattered" used twice. The word in the Greek is *diaspora*. Luke is saying that there is going to be a new diaspora. I call this Diaspora 2.0. The first diaspora referred to the Jewish diaspora when the Jews were scattered over the world due to the Babylonian exile. What is often overlooked about that tragedy is that God actually used the "scattering" of the Jews all over the world to bring the seed of the knowledge of God to distant, remote places. What began as a judgment ended up being a missionary movement. Now, Acts is telling us that there is a new, persecution-driven scattering or diaspora happening. Yet, like the earlier one, it will result in a major spreading of the good news of Jesus

Christ to the ends of the earth. Persecution often spreads the gospel. This story is repeated all across history.

The very fact that the church is now being scattered by persecution reenacts a new kind of exile. We are now being scattered in the world and we have a lot of work to do. God is unfolding a new, global plan of proclamation which, in these early decades of the twenty-first century, continues to unfold.

Power Encounter 2.0

The fact that the apostles stayed in Jerusalem also allowed a new generation of younger leaders to rise up. When Philip gets to Samaria, he encounters Simon the Sorcerer. Philip is not one of the twelve apostles. Now there is a popular theology which many Christians believe known as cessationism. There are a range of views which fall under the general rubric of "cessationism" but one of the dominant streams teaches that the charismatic, or sign, gifts of the Holy Spirit ceased with the apostles. He gave them to the apostles to do miracles—people were being raised from the dead, the blind received sight, etc.—but once the church got launched and the apostles died off, so did the miracles. This text should help to dispel that. In Acts 6, when there was a dispute about the Grecian Jews and Aramaic Jews, the first deacons were appointed. This was a new form of leadership. Seven people were chosen that included Stephen, Philip, Nicanor, Timon, Parmenas, and Nicolas from Antioch. This was a new generation of leadership.

Stephen was martyred for Christ. Philip traveled to Samaria, Jerusalem, and Judea—and the text says that people came to see the miraculous signs that he did. Look at Acts 8:7: "For with shrieks, impure spirits came out of many, and many who were paralyzed or lame were healed." Luke purposely uses the exact language with which he talked about Jesus' ministry—the evil spirits coming out, the shrieking, the healing of paralytics, etc.—to convey what Philip does. Philip is doing the ministry of Jesus in the world, and Philip is not one of the apostles. These are the miracles of Christ that Jesus had promised in John 14:12 when he said that his followers would do even greater works after Jesus went to the Father.

Many people misunderstand what it means for us to do "even greater things" than Jesus. How is that possible? But when he says that we will do "greater things," it is not greater in *power*, it is greater in *scope*. The Holy Spirit takes the localized ministry of Jesus and universalizes it for the whole world. You see, if Jesus was in Bethlehem, he couldn't be in Galilee. If Jesus was in Capernaum, he couldn't be in the Decapolis. As amazing as Jesus' ministry is, it is localized by the human fact of the incarnation. That is why Jesus says that when the Holy Spirit comes, "they will do even greater things than these" (John 14:12), because the particularized ministry of Jesus is universalized through the ministry of the Holy Spirit. The church scatters everywhere and Christ's presence becomes actualized everywhere through the ministry of the Holy Spirit.

Now that the Spirit has come, Philip can be doing the work of Jesus in Samaria while the apostles are back in Jerusalem also doing the work of Jesus. Thus, the Holy Spirit not only enables the ministry of Jesus to continue on in the life of the church, but he is also able to multiple that work through thousands, even millions, around the world. So I call this section of Acts, Power Encounter 2.0. In other words, the power encounter we witnessed in the ministry of Jesus and his disciples is now being passed down to a whole new generation who never personally met Jesus, but who carry his presence and power into the world through the Holy Spirit.

I believe that any miracle that Jesus performed could and should be manifested in the church today. God is always free to act in the world of his making. Any teaching which does not embrace that is, in my view, a deistic view of God. The Deists taught that God is removed from his creation and he does not involve himself in our daily problems and issues. Of course, we should also say that miracles are not the final sign of the authenticity of the gospel. Sometimes, for reasons known only to God, he does not act or heal in the ways we might like him to. Ultimately, the only final authentication of the gospel is that Jesus Christ has come in the flesh and been raised from the dead.

Dr. Craig Keener points out in his commentary on Acts that there is a parallel between Simon the Sorcerer and Philip the Evangelist. They both drew crowds (Acts 8:6, 10). Simon was called "The Great Power of God" (Acts 8:10) and Philip manifested the power of God (Acts 8:7). Simon amazed people; Philip amazed people (Acts 8:9). You see, if the only authentication of truth were miraculous signs and wonders, then many false prophets would be authenticated. What is the difference between Simon the Sorcerer and Philip the Evangelist? It is not simply the signs and wonders in themselves, but it is what they are pointing to. Simon was seeking to advance his own name and recognition. Philp was pointing to and proclaiming Jesus Christ. Simon the Sorcerer was projecting his horizontal vision: he was projecting his own greatness in the world. But Philip was consumed with the glory of God and was only interested in exalting Christ and furthering his kingdom.

Our youngest child, Bethany, has served for more than a decade among an unreached people group called the Alagwa in Tanzania. No crowds are visiting Bethany and giving her special honor and names. Very few are responding to the claims of Christ. There are plenty of demons, but they don't seem to be rushing out when the gospel is preached. There are few who are asking how they might be transformed. When the gospel is preached, most people say no. But the lack of signs and wonders does not erode the fact that God is authentically working there and slowly unfolding his plan for the Alagwa. So, the church should, on the one hand, welcome all signs and wonders. Yet, on the other hand, all Christians should acknowledge that the greatest authentication of the gospel is always Christ himself.

In Bethany's missionary work, she has gotten to know many Alagwa people, and they are at various different stages in their understanding of God and the gospel. However, two of them are very close to becoming public followers of Jesus Christ. One day, they had a scheduled meeting in her home to discuss their faith and whether they were ready to be baptized. They had just started their conversation when a man burst into the room and began shouting curses and denouncing Bethany. The man pushed the two men out of the house and the meeting came to an abrupt end. When Bethany told us this story, we asked her what she was going to do about that man who was so angry and who called down curses upon her? She replied, "Tomorrow, I'm going to spend a day working in this man's field, helping him plant before the rainy season arrives." In that culture there is one main love language, and that is to work in someone's field. And so she went that next day and served the man who had cursed her. Now, that is a great "sign and wonder." Namely, the power of love in the face of hate. The power of forgiveness in the face of broken relationships.

Blessing 2.0

One of the ways the church has spoken of the work of the Holy Spirit in our lives subsequent to our conversion is the phrase "a second blessing." It is a way of setting forth the distinction between the first blessing we receive when we come to Christ and the second blessing we receive when we receive the fullness of the Holy Spirit. I am calling this Blessing 2.0. We can see this twofold blessing unfolding in Acts chapter 8. The apostles in Jerusalem hear about the Samaritans receiving the gospel and getting baptized. In verse 14 it says that many people in Samaria had "received the word of God." This phrase is shorthand for them receiving the message about Christ, which Philip had been proclaiming to them. When the apostles in Jerusalem heard about this, they sent Peter and John down to see it firsthand. When they arrive, they pray that they might receive the Holy Spirit because the Holy Spirit had not yet come upon any of them. They had simply been baptized into the name of the Lord Jesus (Acts 8:15–16).

This is a second work of grace. They have already been baptized in water, but here we have a laying on of hands to receive the Holy Spirit. These are two separate works of God, and there is time and space—and also planning—between the two blessings. Now we have already seen several times in Acts where the Holy Spirit seems to come down spontaneously on new believers. On the day of Pentecost, the Holy Spirit came down in this way. We see this kind of spontaneous outpouring in Acts 2, 8, and 10, where the Holy Spirit comes with no apparent human instrumentality. There was no gap in time. People come to the Lord and they are immediately filled with the Holy Spirit.

At other times there is a clear gap between the two blessings of God. In fact, right in the book of Acts the church develops two separates liturgies, or formal actions, which distinguish these two works of grace. The entrance into the faith is marked by baptism with water. The second work of grace is marked by the laying on of hands. Repeatedly in the book of Acts, the apostles or Paul or other leaders lay hands on people to receive the Holy Spirit.

We have largely lost this wonderful heritage from the New Testament. We have retained the baptism of water, but we have not always retained the practice of the laying on of hands to receive the Holy Spirit. The closest we see this today is when people lay hands on someone to be healed, or to be commissioned for special service. In Acts 8, Philip evangelizes the people of Samaria and baptizes them in water. Later on, Peter and John come down and lay hands on them to receive the Holy Spirit. This is a very important sequence which we should not forget. My point is that receiving the fullness of the Holy Spirit sometimes happens spontaneously according to God's work. Other times, it happens later after some planning and further instruction.[1]

I have gently chided those parts of the church who deny that there even is a second work of grace, but let me also chide our own tradition a bit. One of our problems is that we sometimes think that the only way the Holy Spirit comes upon us is at a "crisis" event when we come to the altar. We might think that if we have a problem in our lives, or some bondage, or a sin, then at some point we need to come forward and have people pray for us.

Now, as we have said, we all need those moments at the altar where God moves in a powerful way in our lives. But, that should never be confused with a *process* whereby you submit to an accountability group and you commit that particular problem to God over time. Sometimes God delivers us dramatically and powerfully through an outpouring of the Holy Spirit. At other times, he works

---

1. The Holy Spirit is active in the lives of unbelievers who alone convicts us of our sin (John 16:8), as well in the lives of all believers who belong to Christ. But, even as Christians, we need to fully surrender to the power and work of the Holy Spirit in our lives if we are to be sanctified (see Ephesians 5:18; Galatians 5:16–17; 2 Corinthians 7:1).

his grace in us by the Holy Spirit over a period of time as we consecrate ourselves to him and learn to submit to him daily in the area where we are struggling. Sometimes our problems are resolved at the altar; sometimes we have struggles which last for decades and we have to continually submit them to the Lord on a daily basis. There is an important role for Christian counselors. And it is certainly advisable for all Christians to be part of some kind of accountability group. You might even consider the counseling session, or the accountability group as another kind of altar. It is not the "crisis" altar, but the "process" altar, and God honors both of them.

Christians love to recount the story of Moses at the burning bush. Now *that* is a crisis event. We all want this, but Moses also spent forty years in the desert of Sinai being purged and prepared for his ministry. We don't talk about that very much. The apostle Paul had a crisis event on the road to Damascus. We have all heard sermons on that. But, rarely do we talk about Paul spending three years in Arabia in the desert before he came back and began his apostolic ministry.

You see, we have to understand that crisis and process are both important for good Christian maturity. We need both the crisis events and the ongoing process. This is why the Holy Spirit is compared to both fire and water. Fire is often used to symbolize quick and dramatic action. Water often symbolizes the slow moving, but powerful force of the Holy Spirit over a long time as he courses his way through our lives. Never confuse the road to Damascus with the deserts of Arabia, or the burning bush with the deserts of Sinai. Jesus Christ had a crisis experience, if there ever was one, at the Jordan River where the Father himself spoke from the sky, and the Spirit himself descended upon him. But then he was sent out into the wilderness to be tempted and prepared for ministry.

After Peter and John encounter the revival breaking out in Samaria, they return to Jerusalem as changed people. This is one of the consistent themes in the book of Acts. God keeps surprising us with his work. Here are the very people that had walked with Jesus, and seen the resurrection and the ascension of Christ. Yet, even they probably felt that they were now seeing the world in color, not just black and white. They left Jerusalem thinking that the gospel was only for the Jews, but they are beginning to realize that God is doing a work far wider and broader than they could have imagined. They are realizing that Jesus is the Lord of the whole world, the desire of every nation.

Six

Tolle Lege, Tolle Lege

Scriptural Background: Acts 8:26–40

In Acts 8:26–40, we have the privilege of witnessing the first convert to Christianity from the African continent. If you go back in history, you will see that since the fourth century, the greatest continent-wide people movements to Christ were the European peoples. The European peoples almost became synonymous with what it meant to be a Christian. People often thought of Christianity as a white person's religion or a part of the European experience. No one could imagine the day when that would change. Yet today, in our lifetime, for the first time in history, the African continent-wide movement to Christ will surpass the number of European peoples who have come to Christ. This is not simply a chapter in church history; this is an epoch in church history. This African movement to Christ can trace it origins to this text with the conversion of the Ethiopian eunuch.

The Conversion of St. Augustine

To lay the foundation for this text, let's look at another African Christian in the year AD 386. At thirty-one, Augustine was already the professor of rhetoric in the great court in Milan, a very prestigious position. He was highly respected and had a promising career ahead of him. But at that particular point, he was living in agony because the intellectual world he had occupied was collapsing. Augustine had spent the previous eight years engulfed in a movement called Manichaeism. It was an intellectually stimulating movement, but had a low regard for the human body. This hindered the movement's ability to make scientific advances (which require that we trust our senses). On top of this, and precisely because this movement had a low view of the body, Augustine had given himself over to all kinds of licentiousness and sensual pleasure. By his own account he was involved in orgies, drunkenness, and illicit sexual behavior. In fact, he had multiple lovers, and even had an illegitimate child.

By the time the year 386 dawned, Augustine had left Manichaeism and had become attracted to the truths of Christianity. But, because he was in bondage to his sensual and sexual pleasures, he was in agony. He went out behind his house and into a garden where he could sit in the grass under a tree. As he sat there, he became very agitated and began to pull his hair out and swing his arms around. He finally got up and went over to a fig tree and fell down on his knees, weeping uncontrollably. In his confessions, he said that he began to cry out the words of Psalm 13: "How long, LORD?"

Have you ever uttered that prayer? Perhaps you have prayed earnestly for an intervention from God. Well, Augustine prayed like that and he received an unusual answer. As he cried out to the Lord, he heard a little voice, like a child's sing-song voice. He later said, "I don't know if it was a boy or a girl. It was clearly children." And they were singing this little phrase, "*Tolle lege, tolle lege.*" *Tolle lege* is Latin for "Take up and read."

This is one of the most important moments of divine intervention in the history of the church. When Augustine heard that, he did not think about the Ethiopian eunuch who had once taken up and read the scroll of Isaiah. Instead, Augustine remembered another famous Christian from Africa known as St. Antony of the desert. Saint Antony is widely regarded as the father of monasticism and was highly revered from the fourth century until today. Saint Antony died when Augustine was only two years old, but as an Algerian, Augustine revered the desert fathers, of whom Antony was the first. In that divine moment in the garden, Augustine remembered that time when Antony had gone through his own excruciating pain and opened the Bible in a moment of crisis. He had fallen upon that text, which said what he needed to hear, "Go, sell your possessions and give to the poor . . . follow me" (Matt. 19:21). Antony had gone out, and one of the great chapters in church history was begun, the start of the monastic movement, which brought together believers under a common rule of life. The most well-known rule of life is known as the Rule of Saint Benedict, which continues in many monastic orders until the present day.

So, when Augustine heard the command, "*Tolle lege, tolle lege,*" (Take up and read, take up and read), he heard it as God's word to him. Augustine opened the Bible and his eyes fell on Romans 13:13–14 (ESV): "Let us walk properly as in the daytime, not in orgies and drunkenness, not in sexual immorality and sensuality, not in quarreling and jealousy. But put on the Lord Jesus Christ, and make no provision for the flesh, to gratify its desires."

We sometimes use the expression "jumping off the page at you." This text seemed to jump off the page at Augustine, just the way it happened to Antony, and as it happened with the Ethiopian eunuch. Augustine realized the huge gap between his life and the holiness of God. This is the second great stream of the Holy Spirit's work in the life of the church: he makes us holy.[2] Augustine was bound in sin and needed to be set free for holy living. This is why conversion cannot be separated from holiness, because this separates the second person of the Trinity from the third person of the Trinity. We are forgiven through the power of Christ, but we are sanctified and made holy by the power of the Spirit.

The book of Acts is committed to an honest assessment of the challenges which the early church faced in regards to holiness. Sometimes we focus so much on the early vitality of the church where thousands are coming to Christ and people are receiving miraculous healings, that we forget

---

2. The three streams, as explained more fully in chapter 2 are: (1) power for global witness, (2) purifying/sanctifying holiness in our lives, and (3) discernment/wisdom for life's journey.

that Acts also shares the obstacles and struggles the early church had with its mission. Among these are internal bickering and fighting (Acts 6:1; 15:2, 37–39) and serious lapses in holiness. Acts 5, for example, highlights the story of Ananias and Sapphira who are set up as a contrast to the earlier declaration that people were selling their land and houses and freely giving the money to the apostles to help serve the poor (Acts 4:34–35). This is where we first meet Barnabus, Paul's later traveling companion. He sold a field he owned and gave the money to the apostles. In contrast, Acts 5 gives us the account of Ananias and Sapphira who conspire together to sell their land and only give a portion of the proceeds to the church. They were, of course, free to sell, or not sell, their land. They would have been free to sell their land and openly declare that they were only giving a portion of the proceeds the church. But, what actually happened was that they sold the land and told the apostles that the money they were giving was actually the full price of the land. This was deception and lying, a clear departure from the call to holy living.

What is fascinating in the account is that when Peter confronts Ananias after he lies, Peter does not accuse him of lying to the leaders of the church. Instead, he asks, "Ananias, why has Satan filled your heart to lie to the Holy

Spirit . . . ?" Later, when Sapphira is confronted, Peter says to her, "How is it that you have agreed together to test the Spirit of the Lord?" (Acts 5:3, 9 ESV). This deception is presented as an affront to the Holy Spirit. Ananias and Sapphira not only lied to the apostles, but they lied to and tested the Holy Spirit. It is clear that the Holy Spirit is highlighted because this is the person of the Trinity whom we associate with the work of sanctification and holiness in our lives. The judgment on both of them was severe (both were struck dead) as a sign of the authority of the Holy Spirit to purge the church of iniquity and make her holy, in anticipation of the great Banquet at the end of time when we, as the Bride of Christ, shall be presented to Christ "in splendor, without spot or wrinkle" (Eph. 5:27 ESV). This is the same passage where Paul commands us all to "be filled with the Spirit" (Eph. 5:18). This verse literally means, "be filled and keep on being filled"[3] with the Holy Spirit. The call to holiness is part of the universal and ongoing call to all believers,

---

3. The Greek word, *plerousthe* (from *pleroo*), used here is a present passive imperative. The present tense implies an ongoing reality of receiving the Spirit, not a one-time action. The imperative mood implies that it is a command, not an option. Finally, the passive implies that it is something God gives to us and we are the joyful recipients of this gift.

whether those in the early church, St. Antony whom the Spirit purged in the deserts of Africa, St. Augustine who was purged of his immorality, or anything we may face today.

Conversion of the Ethiopian Eunuch

As we noted in the last chapter, this passage in Acts comes in that transition part of Acts between Acts 8:1 and Acts 11:19. This is the period in Acts that transitions the church from Jewish fulfillment to Gentile global vision. This is the passage that really begins to drive home the fact that the coming of Jesus is not just about fulfilling Jewish hopes and promises for the Jews, but promises for the whole world. It was difficult for Jews to accept the idea that their Messiah was not just for them, but for the whole world. So, it happens in stages. First (as we saw in the last chapter), it comes to Samaritans who were partially Jewish, but were regarded as heretical and impure. Now, we have the conversion of the Ethiopian eunuch, who had come to Jerusalem to worship. This will be followed by Cornelius's household (who was a God-fearer), and then by Acts 11:10 when the gospel begins to be preached to Gentiles with no connection to Judaism at all.

Spirit Direction #1

In the previous chapter we saw how Philip was used by God to ignite a turn to Christ among the people of Samaria. Now, quite unexpectedly, the Lord directed Philip to leave this move of God and go to the Gaza road. If you look at a map of the time, you will discover that the Gaza road was a lonely, deserted road which connected Palestine with Egypt. People didn't travel that road often, and it was in the middle of the day. In those days people avoided traveling in the heat of the day, so it must have seemed like an odd command to Philip.

Sometimes God calls us away from something we love, and even away from a move of God because he has a new direction in our lives. Perhaps this has happened to you. You were settled in a particular work and, quite unexpectedly, you sensed that God was calling you to something very different.

It happened to George Whitfield in the eighteenth century. God was using him mightily in a revival which would eventually be so big that it would be known as The Great Awakening. Yet, God spoke to George Whitfield and told him to return to America and work there. Whitfield didn't know what to do because he had hundreds of people coming to his meetings and receiving Christ. He didn't see how he could just leave it. But the Lord seemed to be calling him to leave, so he found a young preacher who would step in and continue his work in England. That young preacher was named John Wesley. John Wesley, along with his brother Charles, became God's chosen instruments to continue the work and to solidify the work of the awakening that was taking place. We can look back and recognize the hand of God in this.

The point we should take away from Acts is that God's work is not dependent on any particular person. Luke wants us to know that God himself drives his mission in the world.

Spirit Direction #2

As Philip traveled that lonely road and wondered about all these things, he had a divine moment when he met the eunuch who was the treasurer of the Candace. (Candace is a title for the queen of Ethiopia, though that region was far larger than what we call Ethiopia today. Her name was Amanitore; she served from AD 25 to 41.) This eunuch was her main official who conducted her business and represented her in various places. He was clearly an intelligent, literate, and wealthy person. He had been in Jerusalem, probably as a Gentile God-fearer to pay his respects, worship the Lord, and return home. He was an uncircumcised Gentile. Yet, God directed Philip from Samaria all the way to the chariot that this official was riding in. In Acts 8:29, the Scripture says that the Holy Spirit directed Philip to go up to the chariot.

How many of us have a walk with the Lord which is so close, we can understand and hear it when the Holy Spirit directs us?

Confessions of a Pastor Seeking to Hear the Guidance of the Holy Spirit

Can the Holy Spirit direct you? I have had a number of times where I now know the Holy Spirit directed me to say something in a particular situation or do something and I squelched it. I rationalized my way out of it and I didn't do anything. This is an area where I have been asking God for years to help me grow.

I have had times when I obeyed these promptings. I was in an intensive care unit one time, going to visit one of my parishioners as a part of my normal pastoral duties.

As I exited my parishioner's room, I felt the Holy Spirit say to me, "Go into that IC unit over there and pray with that man." I didn't know who was in that room. I didn't know anything about the person who was laying there. I just sensed that I should go into that unit and pray. I'm really glad I did. The Lord used that encounter not only in the patient's life, but in my life as I became more sensitive to the leading of the Holy Spirit.

I have also had times when I resisted the promptings of the Lord. The best way to grow in this area is to include in your daily prayers a prayer that you might be sensitive to the leading, direction, and promptings of the Holy Spirit for that particular day. I have found that if you go through the day with a heightened sensitivity to the Holy Spirit, you are more likely to not squelch or "grieve" the Holy Spirit by ignoring his voice.

Spirit Direction #3

In this passage in Acts, we find a church driven by the mission of the Holy Spirit. We see this divine moment that God is orchestrating. The eunuch is reading from the scroll of Isaiah, which he probably purchased in Alexandria. The eunuch is from the area of ancient Ethiopia which today would be northern Sudan. Today this is one of the most conflicted places on earth. But, at that time, it was a noble kingdom and respected in the ancient world.

The eunuch is reading from Isaiah 53:7–8 which says:

> "Like a sheep he was led to the slaughter and like a lamb before its shearer is silent, so he opens not his mouth. In his humiliation justice was denied him. Who can describe his generation? For his life is taken away from the earth." (Acts 8:32–33 ESV, quoting Isa. 53:7–8)

Philip overheard him reading this passage from Isaiah and he asked him if he understood the passage. In the original language it is a play on words meaning, "Are you reading, or are you really reading?"[4] The idea is to press whether he is just reading words or if he is really understanding or comprehending. The eunuch invited Philip up into the chariot. Providentially, chapter 53 of Isaiah is one of the four servant songs in Isaiah, arguably the most important messianic passage in the Old Testament. This is

---

4. *Ginoskeis* (reading) or *anaginoskeis* (understanding).

the passage which has so many familiar verses in it, such as "he was wounded for our transgressions" and "with his stripes we are healed" and "all we like sheep have gone astray . . . and the LORD hath laid on him the iniquity of us all" (Isa. 53:5–6 KJV). Luke tells us in the account that Philip started with that passage and "told him the good news about Jesus" (Acts 8:35). We do not know all the passages which Philip used from the scroll to preach Jesus to the eunuch, but since the account mentions six times that this official was a eunuch, perhaps Philip pointed out that passage just a little farther in the scroll which says:

> Let not the foreigner who has joined himself to the LORD say, "The LORD will surely separate me from his people"; and let not the eunuch say, "Behold, I am a dry tree." For thus says the Lord: "To the eunuchs who keep my Sabbaths, who choose the things that please me and hold fast my covenant, I will give in my house and within my walls a monument and a name better than sons and daughters; I will give them an everlasting name that shall not be cut off." (Isa. 56:3–5 ESV)

We don't know for certain what Philip said, or if he used any part of Isaiah other than the one quoted, but it is clear that Philip proclaimed the gospel to the Ethiopian eunuch. The eunuch could not really understand what was being said by Isaiah without the guidance and help of the Holy Spirit through Philip speaking to him.

This is an important theme in Luke's writings, both the gospel of Luke and the book of Acts. Remember the two on the road to Emmaus walking with the Lord Jesus, but not knowing it was him? Luke records that they were "kept from recognizing him" (Luke 24:16) until the time when "their eyes were opened" (Luke 24:31). We see a similar thing when Paul shared the gospel with Lydia outside of Philippi. The text does not simply say that Paul shared the gospel and she responded to the eloquence of Paul and his great insights. Rather, the text says that "the Lord opened her heart to respond to Paul's message" (Acts 16:14). We should never forget that the Lord is the great evangelist.

After Philip preached the gospel, there is a wonderful understatement which appears in the passage. The eunuch says, "See, here is water! What prevents me from being baptized?" (Acts 8:36 ESV). From a Jewish perspective, there were, of course, many reasons why an uncircumcised Gentile could not be baptized. But the Holy Spirit directed Philip to baptize the Ethiopian eunuch, establishing another major step toward the full inclusion of Gentiles which culminates in Acts 11:19–20. It is becoming increasingly clear that the gospel of Jesus Christ is for the whole world, because Jesus died for the sins of the whole world, not just for any particular group. They came upon an oasis of water, so the chariot stopped and the eunuch was baptized. When the eunuch came up out of the waters of baptism, the Holy Spirit snatched Philip thirty miles away to a place called Azotus. Philip continued his evangelistic ministry right up the coast and eventually made his way to Caesarea.

It is in Caesarea that the next major breakthrough happens through the ministry of Peter who is directed by the Spirit to go to the household of Cornelius and preach the gospel. Eventually, when Paul comes to Caesarea toward the end of his third missionary journey, he stays in the home of Philip and his four daughters (see Acts 21:8–9). The underlying message in all of these passages is that the Holy Spirit is directing the mission of the church. It is not based on any human plans or ingenuity, but on being sensitive to the leading of the Holy Spirit.

It is interesting that the text tells us that Philip is "snatched away" (Acts 8:39 NLT). This is the same root word used for the day when the saints are "snatched up" to meet the Lord when he comes back to earth at the end of time (1 Thess. 4:17). It is also used in Corinthians when Paul gets snatched up to meet the Lord in the heavenly vision (2 Cor. 12:2).[5] These instances of God "snatching" people, once again, demonstrates that he is driving the mission of the church.

As we look at the conversion of the Ethiopian eunuch, or the conversion of St. Antony, or the conversion of St. Augustine, or the conversion of the Alagwa, these are all African peoples God is drawing to himself for his glory and purposes in the world. This is part of the grand, God-driven story of redemption which will someday culminate in that great vision of the apostle John who sees in Revelation 7:9 (ESV), "A great multitude that no one could number, from every nation, from all tribes and peoples and languages, standing before the throne" worshiping the Lord.

This is the grand vision in which we are called to participate. It is a Spirit-led, divine mission to fulfill God's original promise to Abraham that in his seed, "all peoples will be blessed" (Gen. 12:3). May each of us be led by the Spirit to participate in the mission of God.

---

5. Translations vary, but the same Greek word is used in all three of these texts. It is the word *arpagenta*, meaning "to seize, catch up, or snatch away."

Seven

The Double Conversion
of the Gospel

*Scriptural Background: Acts 9:3–5,
15–19; 10:23–28, 34–48*

What does a Gamaliel-trained Pharisee named Saul of
Tarsus have to do with a Roman centurion Gentile named
Cornelius? These texts bring together two remarkable
conversions—Saul of Tarsus on the road to Damascus and
the conversion of Cornelius's household. These are the two
most important events in the life of the early church.

Saul was, of course, a Gamaliel-trained Jew. He was the
guy who aced his SAT exam and wondered why everybody
else struggled with it. He was the guy who rose to the top
of everything he did, and very early on, the church learned
that he had risen to the top of those who were out to

destroy the church of Jesus Christ. He had gone to the high priest and received letters of arrest to take to Damascus, and this whole scene on the road to Damascus happened as he was breathing out murderous threats against the church. This was an unbelievably dramatic scene in the life of the church—that someone who was the number-one persecutor would become the apostle to the Gentiles.

Hearing Your Name Twice

It is actually a stock phrase in our culture, and in many cultures in the world, to say someone had a Damascus Road experience. This is probably one of the most profound examples of a complete U-turn of a life that you might ever have encountered. But for a Jewish person reading this, or hearing this passage read, what really would have struck them in the encounter of Christ with Saul of Tarsus was the way he was addressed: "Saul, Saul"—the doubling of the name.

Now, this is something that only happens three times in the Jewish Bible (which is our Old Testament). It happened in Genesis 22, when Abraham was poised to plunge a knife into his son's body. At that point, God intervenes through redemptive history with the doctrine of substitutionary atonement. At that moment, as the knife was raised, God intervened and said, "Abraham, Abraham," and that became the crucial point for the identity and unfolding of the Jewish nation. It happened a second time at the burning bush with Moses. This was the key moment that culminated in the redemptive narrative of the Exodus. Out of the burning bush, God said, "Moses, Moses." The third time it happens is in 1 Samuel 3:10 when Samuel was in the bed and God called him, and said, "Samuel, Samuel." That became the bridge to the prophetic stream, the bridge between the judges and the prophets.

So when the Lord says to Saul, "Saul, Saul," you should hear it like a Mount Moriah moment, a burning bush moment, or a Shiloh moment. This is that kind of remarkable event in the history of God's work. This is bringing us to the gradual transition of the gospel going full throttle to the Gentiles, with no connection to Israel or Judaism at all.

Two Conversion Stories

There are a number of unusual features which make these two conversion stories so remarkable. For example, they are the only accounts in the Bible that come to us three times. Both the conversion of Saul and the conversion of

Cornelius's household are given to us three times. Now, given the general economy of words in the New Testament, this is stunning. Saul's conversion is told in Acts 9, retold in Acts 22 to the crowds, and told again in chapter 26 to Agrippa and Festus. Cornelius's conversion is told in Acts 10, and it is retold in Acts 11 by Peter in Jerusalem, and then again by Peter in Acts 15. Why do you think that these two conversion stories are interwoven into the larger fabric of the book of Acts? There are two major themes which both of these passages help us to understand about God's work. This chapter will focus on these themes.

Collaboration with God in His Mission

The first theme which both texts share is that God calls us to be collaborators with him in the redemption of the world. Now, that is a very important statement, and I hope that you understand how important it is. On the one hand, we all understand that God is sovereign, and this is God's mission, not ours, and he drives it. We've seen that repeatedly in this book. But, on the other hand, God has purposed to include us in his unfolding plan in the world.

Theologically, when we speak of God's sovereignty, and his independent authority to work and freely act, we call this *monergism*. The word *monergism* is built by bringing the prefix "mono" meaning one or alone, together with the word for energy—thus, "one energy." So, monergism is the idea that God is free to act autonomously in the world. He doesn't need our help in redeeming the world. We cannot do things to save ourselves. This is a clear testimony to our utter inability to redeem ourselves or others. The Bible often calls this doctrine the "sovereignty" of God or the "aseity" of God.

But the Bible also speaks of human free will and human responsibility. This teaches us that our actions and decisions really do matter, and that God calls us to action in collaboration with his sovereign will. We call this *synergism*. Synergism speaks of not "one" but "two" energies working together, creating the word *synergy*, or *synergism*. This doctrine, commonly called "free will," emphasizes the other side of the coin; namely, that God does call us to participate with him in his work of redemption. He didn't have to do this, but he chooses to do it. The church has, at times, struggled with keeping both of these truths held in proper tension.

Now, broadly speaking, throughout the history of the church, Roman Catholicism and, in fact, Eastern Orthodoxy as well, are known for being primarily synergistic. During the Reformation in the sixteenth century, the Roman Catholics were regularly accused (and still are to this day), of teaching salvation through works, and a form of works righteousness to the point that the reformers felt that the work of Christ was obscured or buried under the larger emphasis of what we have to do. This was an important point of the tensions which gave rise to the sixteenth-century Reformation. The main Reformation movements (Presbyterians, Lutherans, and Anglicans) are often falsely accused of being passive, teaching that God does everything and that we are not included in either the process of our own salvation or the salvation of others.

One of the analogies which has been used to describe this tension is known as the "kitten/monkey" analogy. If you have ever seen a mother monkey or a mother cat care for their children, you will instantly see why this analogy is used. A mother cat carries her newborn kitten around by the scruff of its neck, and the kitten is completely passive in the process. In contrast, when a baby monkey is carried by its mother, the baby must throw its arms around the mother and cling to her. The "kitten" is the metaphor for monergism, whereas the "baby monkey" is the metaphor for synergism.

Wesleyan theology emerged a century after the Reformation and, by that time, there was a much greater appreciation for the tension between these two doctrines. God's sovereignty and human responsibility in Wesleyan theology are brought together and held in tension as well as any movement in history has done. Wesleyan theology acknowledges that God's sovereignty (including our inability to save ourselves) is taught in Scripture. It also declares that human responsibility (including the need for us to act and decide) is also taught in Scripture. To put this tension another way, Scripture teaches that we are "dead in [our] trespasses and sins" (Eph. 2:1 ESV). Everyone knows that a dead person cannot "do" anything. Yet, Scripture is also filled with verbs that call us to action. The Scriptures call us to repent, to come, to turn, to believe, and so forth. Yet, none of these can be done by people who are spiritually "dead."

Wesley resolved this genuine biblical tension by rediscovering a neglected doctrine which is also taught in Scripture, known as prevenient grace. This refers to a sovereign, universal act of God whereby he gives a measure of universal grace to all people which lifts them up from their depravity and allows them the dignity of making meaningful choices. This doctrine of prevenient grace resolves the tension by embracing the truth of both sides of the equation. We really are dead and depraved apart from the gospel. Yet, God, in his sovereignty, has given us a measure of grace which enables us to respond to him, and thus participate in our salvation, as well as make meaningful decisions which result in the salvation of others. These two conversion stories in Acts powerfully underscore this truth. Amazingly, it is our weak view of the Holy Spirit which has contributed to our struggle in holding these truths together. Let's examine these texts and see how these twin truths intersect with one another.

Acts 9 opens up on the road to Damascus, and is a profound testimony to monergism. Saul has received letters to arrest Christians in Damascus and he was on his way to execute the new warrant. However, God sovereignly inter-vene in the life of Saul of Tarsus. God is the acting subject; Saul is the object of this. God confronted Saul unilater-ally on the road to Damascus. This is abundantly clear in the text. What is interesting, however, is not so much what happened on the road to Damascus, but what did *not* happen there. Here is Jesus, the Baptizer of the Holy Spirit, who did not baptize or fill Saul on the road to Damascus. Saul was not filled with the Spirit as we witnessed on the day of Pentecost. In fact, it is never even brought up.

Saul was only left blinded on the road to Damascus, which is a way of conveying that Saul could not have thought his way to the gospel. He was utterly helpless before God. Saul was a Gamaliel-trained Jew, brilliant by every account, steeped in the Law, steeped in the Word of God, but he could not think his way to the gospel. He needed a divine intervention. Saul of Tarsus could not do this.

God then turned to an unknown believer at the time named Ananias and commanded him to become involved. Ananias struggled with the prompting because he was afraid. But the Scripture highlights the importance of Ananias's action and, amazingly, Ananias became a key instrument in Paul's infilling and empowering for apostolic ministry.

Ananias was told to pray for Paul to receive the Holy Spirit. Ananias was told, "Go, for he is a chosen instrument of mine to carry my name before the Gentiles and kings and the children of Israel" (Acts 9:15 ESV). Later when Paul recounted his conversion, he said that it was the risen Lord who proclaimed this to him (Acts 26:16–18). The point is, this is not a contradiction; it's the same thing. Paul received Ananias's commission as if from the Lord himself. God and Ananias were working together to bring Saul of Tarsus to both justifying and sanctifying grace, the work of Christ and the filling of the Holy Spirit. Ananias was God's agent, working in collaboration with him.

In a similar way, an angel appeared to Cornelius. It is a divine interruption, almost like the Damascus road. Now, you would think that if God sent an angel all the way from heaven to Cornelius's house, the angel would go ahead and preach the gospel to Cornelius. But the angel did not do that. Instead, the angel simply told Cornelius to bring Peter to his home and listen to whatever Peter tells him. Thus, like Ananias, Peter was divinely pulled into the salvation event of Cornelius's household. The angel appearing to Cornelius, and the risen Lord appearing to Saul on the road to Damascus are both testimonies to monergism, or God's sovereignty. But the inclusion of Ananias and Peter in the conversion of Saul of Tarsus and of Cornelius's household are powerful testimonies to synergism.

God introduces human instrumentality and collaboration into the story. This is one of the important themes which ties these two passages together. Indeed, this theme is found throughout the post-resurrection period and the book of Acts. We see God's sovereignty in John 20, Acts 2, and Acts 4, where God acts independently. But, we also see important places of human instrumentality in Acts 8 (Peter and John coming down to pray for the people of Samaria), in Acts 9 (the inclusion of Ananias), and in Acts 10 (the inclusion of Peter).

Throughout this whole process, we are learning about the dignity of our participating with God in his work. The Reformation had as their primary metaphor that of a condemned sinner desperately running to the cross of Christ. This is a powerful and true picture of what it means to be justified through the sovereign work of God. But, less emphasis was placed on what happens to us *after* we flee to the cross. The Holy Spirit equips us to become collaborators with God and we are joined with others who are "in Christ" and who are now part of the community of the faithful who work together to serve Christ and to extend his kingdom.

The challenging thing is that once we truly become sharers with Christ in his work of redemption, we also become participants in his sufferings. When Saul of Tarsus is saved and called into full-time work as an evangelist and church planter, the Lord says, "I will show him how much he must suffer for the sake of my name" (Acts 9:16 ESV). Thus, the collaboration with God means not only being united with him in the work of redemption, but also being united with him in his rejection and his suffering in the world.

Finally, just to be clear, when we say that we are collaborators with God, we are using the prefix "*co*," not as meaning *equal*, like co-chairs of a committee. The triune God is sovereign and he alone directs the mission of the church. The word "collaboration" is used only to indicate that in his sovereign plan he has graciously chosen to *allow us to participate with him* in his work. We are summoned in his mission and his work of redeeming the world. It is always his mission. He alone is the sovereign God. But he does include us.

Double Conversion

The second theme in these two texts which binds them together is what I call the double conversion of the gospel. What does this mean? This means that not only is the person who hears being transformed by the gospel, but so is the person who is sharing the gospel.

In the Cornelius account, Peter has a vision of a sheet with all kinds of clean and unclean animals in it, and he is commanded to "kill and eat" (Acts 10:13). Peter refuses because it would be a violation of the Jewish dietary restrictions. But this vision happens three times, and then Peter meets the delegation who have arrived and are asking him to come to Cornelius's household, a family of Gentiles. The Spirit tells him to go with them (Acts 10:19–20). Peter himself, after the conversion of Cornelius, declares what he understood the vision to have meant: it was not really about clean and unclean foods, but it was about *people*. After Peter arrived in Cornelius's household and ate with them, a violation of Jewish customs, Peter said to them, "God has shown me that I should not call anyone impure or unclean" (Acts 10:28). In other words, Cornelius's household was transformed by the gospel, but so was Peter! Peter and Cornelius were both converted. Cornelius was converted and now believes the gospel. Peter already believed the gospel, but he is "converted" into realizing that the gospel is much bigger than he realized. Cornelius was converted into the faith; Peter was converted into the full scope of the faith. Peter's faith was already present, but now it is enlarged, and he realizes the full scope of the gospel.

When we share the gospel, it is not just those to whom we witness who are changed, but we, too, are also changed by the encounter. This is why the earlier point about collaboration is so important. If God had not chosen to include Peter in the story, and instead had told the angel to preach the gospel to Cornelius, we would only end up with one saved family. But, by drawing Peter into the story, we end up with two transformed people, and a path opened for the inclusion of all the Gentiles. Indeed, it is Peter's transformation which is the main reason Luke included this in his account in Acts. Because this is the larger story which Luke is sharing with us; namely, how the gospel went from being a fulfillment of Jewish hopes to the hope of all nations.

The same is true in the account of Saul's conversion on the road to Damascus. If God had sovereignly brought everything to Saul that he needed for his salvation and empowering for ministry, we would end up with one saved man on a mission. But by bringing Ananias into the picture, we have a double conversion. Saul is converted to the Christian faith, and Ananias is "converted" to a broader understanding of the scope of the gospel and the astounding power of God's grace to change an enemy of the gospel into an apostle.

By bringing Ananias and Peter into his unfolding drama, God raises up a whole new community who realize the fullness of God's redemptive intentions. Indeed, once the church began to grow among Gentiles, it increasingly became clear that this new community had to be called by a new name. They were originally called "the way" (Acts 9:2), referring to a particular subset of Judaism who believed that Jesus was the Messiah. But it is after the breakthrough in Antioch (Acts 11:19–24) that they began to be called "Christians." This was only possible because of the "double conversions" which were taking place as God summoned Jews to a front-row seat to see and participate in his work, knowing that they would also be changed by what they saw and witnessed.

I have served as the president of Asbury Theological Seminary for more than ten years. The whole purpose of my coming to Asbury is to help this community to further its mission. God has blessed Asbury during this season and I am thankful for it. But, the last ten years have also been a time when I have been transformed through serving in this capacity. That's the way God works. Many of us may feel reluctant to answer God's call to something. We may feel inadequate. But the grace of God always meets us and transforms us along the way. I did not have, in my own reservoir, the capacities to be the president of a seminary. But, by saying yes to God's clear call, he graciously gave me the capacities to do what he had called me to do.

God may be calling you to a new and challenging season in your life. You may sense a genuine inadequacy to answer his call. But, if you submit to God's plan, he will provide, and like he did for Peter and Ananias of long ago, he will enlarge your faith and allow you to live into whatever he may be calling you to do.

C. S. Lewis once said, "God whispers to us in our pleasures, he speaks in our consciences, but He shouts in our pain. It is His megaphone to rouse a deaf world."[6] I want to amend it to include this: it is also his megaphone to rouse a deaf church. The church is in an unhealthy place today. We need a whole new generation of Christians to, symbolically speaking, roll up their sleeves, put on their boots, and get to work. The Lord is calling leaders who will collaborate with God in the building up of his body, the church. We ourselves will be transformed and enlarged in our capacities to serve and love like Jesus as we do, and the world will see more of the true glory and power of the Christian gospel. Are we prepared to take those steps and to fully participate in God's unfolding, redemptive plan?

---

6. C. S. Lewis, *The Problem of Pain* (New York: Macmillan, 1944), 91.

Eight

The Spirit-Directed Church

Scriptural Background: Acts 13:1–3; 16:6–10

Have you ever really wanted to know God's will and you were prepared to do it, but you didn't have a clue what it was? To put it more bluntly, have you ever thought, *I really want to do God's will, but why won't he just tell me what it is?* I mean, why does God seem to be so silent before a willing servant? Many of us struggle with God's will, and maybe even would say, "If we're willing to do God's will, it seems like he owes us the courtesy to at least tell us what it is." Perhaps you have felt like that.

The four spiritual laws[7] are the most well-known evangelistic tract of the twentieth century. The first law is: "God loves you and offers a wonderful plan for your life." I'm sure that's true, but how in the world do you know what that wonderful plan is? Guidance is a really important thing. I realize that in a larger sense, God's will is to conform all of us to the image of Christ. But, on a more particular level, how do you live into that vocationally? How do you know God's will for your life? And how are you to use your life for his kingdom? These are really important questions that most everybody struggles with at some point in his or her life.

Popular Ways of Knowing God's Will in Your Life

In my struggle to understand all of this, I have found that Christians have very different kinds of advice when

---

7. The four spiritual laws are: 1. God loves you and offers a wonderful plan for your life. 2. Man is sinful and separated from God. Therefore, he cannot know and experience God's love and plan for his life. 3. Jesus Christ is God's only provision for man's sin. Through him you can know and experience God's love and plan for your life. 4. We must individually receive Jesus Christ as Savior and Lord; then we can know and experience God's love and plan for our lives.

it comes to knowing God's will. The first is what I would call the *needle-in-the-haystack* view. These aren't the official, professional terms; these are just my own ways of describing these views. This view says that God has one fixed will for your life and your job is to find it. It conceptualizes God's will as very difficult to find. It's like finding the needle of God's will in the haystack of all the distractions of the world, the flesh, and the devil that come roaring through your life; and it's a great recipe for discouragement.

If you know the teaching around this view, many fine distinctions are made which make the discovery of God's will for your life even more challenging. God's "perfect" will is that proverbial needle in the haystack. But, you may actually be in another lower tier, such as God's "preferential" will, or his "perceptive" will, or his "permissive" will. I never knew how to find out which "p" I was on—so I just hoped I was on the right one.

Second, there is the *elephant-in-the-room* view. This view is the opposite of the first. This view says that God's will is right before your eyes all the time. Just get up and do it. You don't need any mystical experience or special invitation; you just need to seize the day. This view is summarized by the phrase, "the need constitutes the call." If you see hungry people, you don't need to spend time praying about helping them. If you have the ability to feed them, then feed them. If you see people who need evangelism and you have the ability to evangelize, then just do it. But many of you will see all kinds of needs that you can throw yourself into, and you may have gifts for an endless array of Christian needs. There are endless good things to do and ways to serve God. How do you know which one to choose and devote your life energy to? What do you do if the elephant in the room becomes a herd of elephants?

The third view is the *follow-your-passion* view. This is where you get all the spiritual inventory websites. These inventories are like the Christian version of Myers-Briggs. Through these tests, you find out what your gifts and inclinations are. If you are gifted with raising awareness for human-trafficking, then you should do that. If you're gifted at preaching the gospel, you should do that. If you're gifted at administration, there's a school waiting to receive your gifts.

But many of you have multiple gifts. And many of you have gifts you have yet to even discover that you have. It may take decades to fully realize some of the gifts God has given to you. Furthermore, sometimes God calls us to areas that don't really fit our inclinations or gifts, and he surprisingly equips us in ways we would have never dreamed.

In previous chapters we have discussed the primary channels through which the Holy Spirit works, including the Spirit's power to bring the gospel to the ends of the earth, and the purifying work of the Holy Spirit. The third channel, which we have not focused on as much, involves the Holy Spirit, who works in wisdom, discernment, and guidance in our lives. This will be the theme of this chapter.

In the midst of Paul's missionary journey, we find out a lot about God's guidance in Paul's life and in the life of the church in Antioch which commissioned and sent out Paul and Barnabus. Interestingly, if you look at these texts carefully, none of them fit into the needle-in-the-haystack, elephant-in-the-room, or follow-your-passion views. We see some very different ways in which God's will was discerned in the New Testament. Perhaps all of this deserves a deeper look.

The Church in Antioch

In Acts 11:19–21, we are introduced to the church of Antioch, planted by those unnamed disciples from Cyprus and Cyrene. Let's explore some of the features of the church in Antioch.

Antioch is a church that exercises spiritual gifts.

In Acts 13, the church has matured and they are exercising spiritual gifts. In this passage, we meet prophets, pastors, and teachers in this church. If you look at the four lists of spiritual gifts in the New Testament found in Romans 12, 1 Corinthians 12, and the two lists found in Ephesians, we see that only one gift is found on all four lists: the gift of prophecy. Right in the book of Acts we see that this young church already has prophets present. Now in the Scriptures a prophet is not limited to those who foretell the future. That, of course, does happen. But more often, a prophet is someone who forth-tells—which means someone is gifted to explain or proclaim God's Word, and give guidance and direction for the church. In other words, prophets are crucial to knowing God's will. The gift of prophecy is one of God's provisions designed to help the church understand and know his will.

Antioch is a church with diversity.

The second thing we notice about the church in Antioch is that it is very diverse. There are three kinds of diversities in this church that I want to highlight. First of all, we have ethnic diversity represented by Barnabas, Simeon called Niger, Lucius of Cyrene, and Manaen, who grew up in Herod's household. By examining the names and the few clues in the opening verses, we know that this group includes Jews and Gentiles in leadership, with diversity in economics and education. We also see geographic and cultural diversity. Not one of the leaders mentioned in Acts 13 is even from the same country. None of them are from Antioch. In fact, they are from five different countries that include Cyrene, Cyprus, North Africa, Turkey, and Jerusalem. This provides a glimpse of the global vision of the church.

Antioch is a Spirit-directed church.

Third, the church of Antioch is a Spirit-directed church. While they are worshiping the Lord and fasting, the Holy Spirit gives guidance to the church gathered together. Now we often think about discerning God's will as a personal struggle. Here, we see the Spirit of God speaking corporately to the church with a prophetic gift. The Holy Spirit instructs the church to set apart Saul and Barnabas for the work to which God was calling them.

Think about how challenging this must have been for the church at Antioch. They are the fastest-growing church in the world, and by the close of the second century, the Christians in this region will number a quarter of a million believers, making it the one of the leading hubs in the growing Christian movement. Antioch is also important because it was here that the first Gentiles who had no prior connection to Judaism as proselytes or God-fearers had come to faith in Jesus Christ. Antioch also had a kind of "dream team" pastoral staff. Their lead pastors were the apostle Paul, the greatest theologian the church has ever known, and Barnabus, who had such strong pastoral skills that he was known as "the son of encouragement." Yet, one night at their prayer meeting, the Holy Spirit speaks and says, "Send out Saul and Barnabas for the work to which I have called them to." They were being led to send both of their pastors out to plant new churches. That had to have been challenging for them. But, we are discovering that the nature of the church is always to be pressing out to new places and among new peoples as we plant the church afresh in every community.

The Birth of the Missionary Band

The church in Antioch was being called to bring the gospel to new, distant places. The problem with this is that the nature of any church is that it is located in a particular place. A church doesn't change locations week after week. A new structure was needed which would allow the church at Antioch to extend their witness and ministry to other places. The result was the birth of the missionary band, a small mobile group who were free to travel from place to place and focus on evangelism and church planting. This is the "spiritual direction" they received from the Holy Spirit. This new structure (not a church structure, but a missionary structure) is what unleashed a massive advance of the church. This separate structure, Paul's missionary band, was able to plant churches in Cyprus, Antioch, Iconium, Lystra, Derbe, Philippi, Thessalonica, Berea, Athens, Corinth, and Ephesus, which form the spine of church growth in the book of Acts.

The church at Antioch itself could not plant any of those churches because their structure, as I noted, was fixed to one location. But the mobile, missionary structure had the flexibility to do this. Thus, the real breakthrough of Acts 13 is not just the calling of two gifted individuals, but a whole new structure that will allow the church to rapidly spread to new places.

You have probably heard about the Asbury College revival of 1970, one of the great revivals of the twentieth century. But, if you actually look at the history of the Asbury revival, the reason it became known as the Asbury revival and spread across this country is because someone had the foresight to realize that the revival would be limited if it just stayed in Wilmore, Kentucky. They created a secondary structure, and they actually created bands of students who went out from Wilmore and traveled all over the country, sharing what God was doing in Wilmore—and revival broke out there as well.

You can see that the church structure and the traveling band-type structure are both crucial for the way the church expands. This was actually the original purpose of the itinerancy system in the Methodist world. If you look at the early days, all itinerancy was designed to spread the church, evangelize, and plant new churches. Sadly, the original design of the itineracy has been largely lost and, in its place, it has become what one United Methodist pastor has called, "a temporary chaplaincy and promotions system."

One of the great legacies of Asbury Theological Seminary is its emphasis on church planting. Today we are particularly challenged because in order to reach millennials for Christ, we have to go to where they are and start churches in some very unusual places. I have made a list of some of the places where Asbury Seminary graduates have planted churches in just the last few years. We have planted churches in coffeehouses, in pubs, community centers, theaters, homes, school cafeterias, Home Depot break rooms, public parks, tattoo parlors, and I'm sure, many more. To me this shows the vibrancy of what happens through the guidance of the Holy Spirit.

In Acts 15:36, Paul suggests to Barnabus that they launch a second missionary journey since the first had been so successful. However, the two enter into a dispute over whether to include John Mark as part of the team, and they end up separating, with Barnabus taking John Mark, and Paul taking Silas. This must have been an unsettling experience—to have God so clearly calling them to go out as a team, and yet, to be in such sharp disagreement that they have to separate. As it turns out, this is just the beginning of the problems Paul encounters in his second journey. In Acts 16, we find Paul traveling through the region of Galatia, and then we are told that he is "forbidden by the Holy Spirit to speak the word in Asia" (Acts 16:6 ESV). Then, they try to enter Mysia and Bithynia and "the Spirit of Jesus would not allow them" (Acts 16:7). In chapter 13, they had clearly been called into this mission, but now in chapter 16, they are finding nothing but closed doors.

It is very easy in the face of a closed door to doubt the original call of God. Have you ever been there? I've been there. It's very easy to forget in the dark what you learned or heard in the light. Paul and his missionary band have this experience, and they are at a loss as to what to do. They don't know what the next step should be.

I have been in this situation. One of the things I learned through those trials is the knowledge that even when God says "no" and all the doors seem to be closing, in the long run, God's "no" is always a deeper "yes." If we are patient, God will, in time, reveal his plan, and it is always a better, deeper plan for us that better fulfills his mission and calling in our lives.

This happens to Paul and his missionary band. They have all these closed doors, but then Paul gets a vision of a Macedonian man beckoning them to come over and help them. The "no" of separation and closed doors becomes, over time, the deeper "yes" of the Macedonian call, and the emergence of Silas as an important new leader in the life of the church.

Once they cross over into Europe in response to the Macedonian call, they meet a woman named Lydia in

Philippi. She and her household become the first Christians in Europe. Very quickly though, Paul finds himself arrested, and both Paul and Silas are thrown into prison. Think about it. Paul and Barnabas supernaturally receive God's call to form the first missionary band, but it eventually ends up in division and sharp disagreement. In the second mission, they determine to bring the gospel farther than ever before, but at each point the Holy Spirit seems to close the door. Then, finally, they get direction about going to Philippi, but very quickly find themselves arrested and thrown into prison. Although it must have been difficult to see God's way through this, their experience in prison becomes God's greater "yes," because after the earthquake, the jailer and his whole family come to Christ.

But still, the difficulties continue. Paul finds an open door in Thessalonica, but when he gets there a mob tries to kill him. He has to escape in the middle of the night to Berea. As the apostles travel from town to town, not always by their choice, they keep spreading the gospel. The mob follows Paul to Berea, so he escapes to Athens. But none of his companions could join him there, so he's left alone in Athens. He finally makes it to Corinth where he meets huge opposition. Finally, the Lord appears to Paul in Acts 18:9–10, saying, "Do not be afraid, but go on speaking and do not be silent, for I am with you, and no one will attack you to harm you, for I have many in this city who are my people" (ESV).

That is a great and powerful assurance from the Lord about his calling in the life of Paul. But, there is a lot of turbulence between Acts 16 and Acts 18. Some of you who are reading this may be experiencing life between Acts 16 and Acts 18. You know that God has spoken to you in the past, and he has given you guidance and a sense of direction. But now you are experiencing spiritual turbulence. Perhaps you have come up against closed doors. You probably have not been thrown into prison for your faith, but there are times when maybe you feel like you have. The Bible tells us that all of God's promises are "yes" in Jesus Christ (2 Cor. 1:20). Our greatest disappointments can become his appointment. Part of the life of faith is persevering through the difficulties, knowing that God is actually using his call, and even the difficulties, to form us and shape us.

The New Testament Practice of Understanding and Knowing God's Will

There are three big takeaways from these passages as we think about the Spirit's guidance in our lives. First, in the

New Testament, the gathered church clearly plays a much stronger role in discerning God's will than we have realized. Do we have a place for the church to speak into our lives? When the apostles had the vision of the Macedonian man, they still met together and decided that it must be God's will for them to go to Philippi. Second, we have to do a better job persisting through roadblocks and various closed doors that we meet which shout "no" to us. The book of Acts models this. We must be persistent in God's call. And, finally, we need much greater openness to the ministry of the Holy Spirit. The prophetic gift is greatly neglected. I haven't been to many churches that have nurtured the prophetic gifts, yet this is one of the key gifts in the New Testament, and it did not die out with the apostles.

Personal Testimony

I'd like to share a little of my own experience as I struggled to know God's will for my life, and the life of my family. In the late 1970s, I felt that God was calling me into full-time ministry. I could only interpret that as a calling into a lifetime of pastoral ministry. Eventually, I came to see that my calling was expanded to include ministry in higher education, but that took place only through a lot of struggle.

In 1990, I sensed God calling us to a new ministry of missionary work which was reaching Muslims for Christ in Nigeria. I was sure that God had called us to Nigeria to be a part of this work. I resigned from my pastorate and we prepared to go to Nigeria. I went to Nigeria ahead of the family to find a house and get things set up because our children were small. Once I arrived in Nigeria, there was a failed coup in the country and, to make a long story short, I was told I had to immediately vacate the country. I had spent a transitional year preparing for that mission by getting a master of theology in Islam at Princeton, and had written my thesis on the practice of Islam in Nigeria. But all of that came crashing down. I returned to our little apartment in Princeton with no job, no clear direction, and a lot of questions.

I remember one night telling my wife, Julie, that I could absorb all of these disappointments if God would just tell me why he was putting us through all of this. I remember Julie quietly reminding me that we were God's servants, and that he didn't owe us an explanation. The Holy Spirit was preventing me from going to Nigeria.

Eventually, I received a call from my district superintendent in Georgia, who said that he was prepared to appoint me to a church. He mentioned four possible churches he might send me to. I told him that I would gladly serve any of the four churches he mentioned.

When the appointments were finalized, I was not sent to any of those four, but we were sent to Carnesville, Georgia. It was a tiny town. When I told my praying friends at Princeton that we were going to Carnesville, Georgia, they laughed and said, "That sounds like a truck stop on I-85." When we got there, we realized that Carnesville was, in fact, a truck stop on I-85. I did not know how to make sense of God's unfolding will in my life. I had a dream of planting churches among Muslims in Nigeria, and here I was at a truck stop on I-85.

My discouragement was compounded when we pulled up at the Methodist parsonage. I got out of the truck and knocked on the door of the parsonage. The leader of the Pastor-Parish Relations Committee, a man named T. C. Lockerman, came to the door. He had never met us; all he knew was that the pastor was arriving with two children. He said to me, "Hello son, where is your father?" I realized that he thought I was too young to be the pastor. He must have concluded that I was one of the pastor's children. I had the painful job of telling him that, actually, I *was* his new pastor.

That night, I remember crying out to God and asking him why I had ended up in Carnesville, and if I missed God's voice which had so clearly seemed to be leading us to Nigeria. The Lord spoke to me in my anguish and said something to me that I will never forget. He said, *"If you can't serve me here, I can't use you anywhere; but if you can serve me here, I can use you everywhere."* It was a defining moment for me to realize that I was caught up in the larger plan of God even though it made no sense to me. It turns out that Carnesville is only a few miles from Toccoa Falls College where I eventually began to teach, and that is how I transitioned into full-time teaching. I had to go to Nigeria and back to learn a basic lesson of God's call: persevere in your calling. When you face closed doors, learn to persevere until you discover the deeper "yes" behind the "no."

The reason I think we struggle with God's will is not so much because we are not spiritual enough, or because we have not prayed enough about it. It is more likely linked to the fact that we do not have a sufficiently mature church which is listening closely to the Lord and can speak God's will into our lives. It is also quite likely that we may have become discouraged by a closed door, or two or three of them, and have not persisted in God's call. Always remember God's call, even in the darkest days. Finally, our theology of the Holy Spirit is too weak, and we do not exercise the gift of the Spirit speaking to us. The gift of prophecy needs to be revived. We need to hear the Spirit more, not less, in our churches. So, perhaps it is time to think differently about how to discern God's will and how God's guidance happens in our lives.

Nine

Twelve Men and a Question

Scriptural Background: Acts 18:24–28; 19:1–7

I have made some really stupid statements in my life. How about you? One of mine occurred around 1983 when I said to my father-in-law, "I have no interest in watching any black-and-white films because all of the really good films are in color." Now, in my defense, I grew up with only black-and-white TV, and I experienced the days when films were, for the first time, coming out in color. I was enchanted by the powerful images of a color movie. Julie's dad, lovingly, like Pricilla and Aquila of long ago, "pulled me aside and explained" the world of film more adequately to me. He asked me if I had seen *The Bells of St. Mary*, or

Sergeant York, or *Twelve Angry Men,* and I had to sheepishly admit that I had never seen any of those movies. So, he began to introduce me to some of the great, classic black-and-white films of his generation. Many of them I now consider, in my more enlightened state, to be true classics, and I love them all.

One of my favorites is *Twelve Angry Men,* starring Henry Fonda, which is the story of a jury that is all too ready to convict a man who was actually innocent of murder based purely on a mountain of circumstantial evidence. Henry Fonda, who plays the lead role, was the sole vote of "not guilty" in the first round of the twelve-man jury. The entire movie is framed around the question that he keeps posing, *"Is it beyond a reasonable doubt?"* Throughout the film, which completely takes place in the jury room, each vote is gradually changed until the man is correctly found innocent.

A Key Question

I thought about that movie when I reread this text in Acts 19 about twelve men, not in a jury room, but in a little house church in Ephesus, who were asked that penetrating question: "Did you receive the Holy Spirit when you believed?" It is one of the most important questions in the life of the church, but one that Christians are only rarely ever asked. In my own experience, the question raised in Acts 19 happened in my own life in 1977. I was in college at the time, and there was a renewal movement sweeping the nation which was drawing attention to the role of the Holy Spirit in the life of the believer.

I think this spiritual awakening can arguably be traced back to the Asbury revival which took place in Wilmore, Kentucky, in February of 1970. The Asbury revival was probably just one chapter in a larger story but, without a doubt, the church at that time was being confronted in a very powerful way with this question: "Did you receive the Holy Spirit when you believed?"

I had experienced a powerful conversion to Christ in 1975, but no one ever asked me when I came to Christ, "Did you receive the Holy Spirit when you believed?" Like the Ephesian believers, I hadn't really heard about the Holy Spirit. I was Trinitarian in a vague theological sense, but had no real understanding of the work and ministry and power of the Holy Spirit in my own life.

But in 1977, in the midst of this renewal wave sweeping the country, I was asked that question. In fact, I remember the exact day I was asked that question for the first time. It was September 25, 1977. I remember it because I had just turned eighteen the day before, and the day before that, I had been elected president of my class in college. My mind was caught up in all those things when, like a lightning bolt lighting up the night sky, I was asked, "Did you receive the Holy Spirit when you believed?" That question cracked a door in my life which, like the Henry Fonda movie of long ago, eventually led me to reconsider my Christian experience, and to be open to a new direction. The fact was, that I really had not received the Holy Spirit when I believed—at least not in his fullness.

The text in Acts 19 is not without difficulties. One of the most intriguing questions is whether or not these twelve believers in Ephesus were followers of Jesus who simply had deficient knowledge about the Christian message and needed to be brought more fully into a faith they already had, or whether they were followers of John the Baptist and needed to be brought into the faith altogether. The larger context of this short passage is that we are in Paul's third missionary journey, which began in Acts 18:23. Right off the bat, we encounter two passages of people who are deficient in their Christian experience. First, we meet Apollos in Corinth. Then, we meet the twelve believers in Ephesus.

Apollos

Apollos was a Jew from Alexandria who was also in this in-between world between being a follower of John and a full-fledged follower of Jesus. We actually know a bit more about Apollos than we do the twelve disciples in Ephesus. Apollos is given five accolades in the text. First, we are told in Acts 18 he was "eloquent" (v. 24 ESV). Second, he had a "thorough knowledge" of the Scriptures (v. 24). Third, he was instructed (or catechized) in the way of the Lord (v. 25). Fourth, Apollos was "fervent in spirit," meaning fervent in *his* spirit, not fervent in the Holy Spirit (v. 25 ESV). Finally, he was earnest and bold in both his teaching and his preaching (v. 26). Yet, despite all of these accolades, the question comes to him (and to all of us): "Did you receive the Holy Spirit when you believed?" (Acts 19:2). Some of you who are reading this are very gifted. You may also be eloquent and fervent. But, the question still finds its way to us: "Did you receive the Holy Spirit when you believed?"

Apollos is shown in the text to have a deficiency in his theology and his experience because he only knew the baptism of John (18:25). This is why Priscilla and Aquila took him aside and explained things to him more adequately about the fullness of Jesus. It is significant that prior to this he only knew about the "way of the Lord."

Thus, there are intentional and clear parallels between Apollos and the twelve disciples who both seem to be in similar situations, having knowledge of John's message and baptism, but lacking a full understanding of—if I might quote our tradition—"the whole Bible for the whole world." In this case, the defining question is: "Did you receive the Holy Spirit when you believed?" Because that, my friends, is one of the defining questions which clearly identifies a deficient Christian experience, whether for a pre-Christian earnest seeker, or for a believer who embraces Jesus but does not have the infilling and empowerment of the Holy Spirit. There are many defining Wesleyan doctrines, but certainly the crown of them all is the insistence that biblical salvation cannot be reduced to the work of Christ, as central as that is; but that biblical salvation involves all three persons of the Trinity. The Father elects us and calls us, the Son redeems us and justifies us, and the Spirit empowers and purifies us.

Who Are These Believers in Ephesus?

So let's take a closer look at this little band of believers in Ephesus. *First, we are told that they were disciples.* We are told in Acts 19:1 that when Paul arrived he "found some disciples." It doesn't say whether they were disciples of John or disciples of Jesus. The word "disciples" is used by itself eleven times in Luke and twenty-one times in Acts, and in every case it clearly refers to Christian believers, so just the generic term "disciple" does not mean that they are only disciples of John. The three times Luke refers to John's disciples, he qualifies it by saying John's disciples or the disciples of John (Luke 5:18; 7:33; 11:1). We don't have any evidence external to the New Testament that there were persistent bands of followers of John the Baptist scattered around the ancient world. On the other hand, how could a follower of Christ not know about or have experienced the baptism of Jesus? Surely, by all accounts, baptism in the name of Jesus is the most fundamental and initiatory liturgical rite in the life of the church.

Bounded Set vs. Centered Set and the Fullness of the Gospel

First, the question—*Are the twelve believers in Ephesus followers of John who need to be brought to Christ, or followers of Jesus who need better instruction?*—may depend on whether the underlying premise assumes what we call a "bounded set" or assumes a "centered set." A bounded set is where the word *Christian* has very strict boundaries—you are either "in" or "out," based on certain defining things which move you across a boundary from "non-Christian" to "Christian." If that is the assumption, then there may very well be a real distinction between Apollos and the twelve Ephesian "disciples."

If, however, the same question is framed as a centered set, then what you have are two situations, Apollos and the Ephesian disciples, who are both on a journey *toward* Jesus. Jesus is the center and the goal of the journey, and people are at different places in the journey. We may not know if and when any particular line is crossed between "Christian" and "non-Christian." In a more Christianized world, bounded-set thinking is not only predominant, but actually may be useful. But in a non-Christian context, or a mission field context, a centered-set understanding is more appropriate.

Second, *note that there are twelve of them.* This clearly should call to mind the number of the original twelve disciples, underscoring the point that the original apostolic band is being reproduced through the mission of the church. We saw this with the transition from the ministry of the Twelve in the opening of Acts; to the ministry of the first deacons, particularly Stephen and Philip and then, in the ministry of the unnamed disciples from Cyprus and Cyrene. It is showing that the ability to convey the Holy Spirit does not die out with the disciples.

Third, *they had only received the baptism of John.* Actually, it really does not matter whether these are disciples of John, and not actually Christians yet. They are on the journey toward Jesus Christ. The point is that you can be a follower of Jesus, whether as a pre-Christian moving toward Christ, or (as with the believers in Samaria), a Christian who is simply deficient in your understanding and your experience. There are many ways in which we can be theologically deficient (the thief on the cross had simple faith in Jesus, which was sufficient, but there is so much more fullness awaiting all believers). There are even more ways in which we can be deficient in our Christian experience. It might be in our prayer life, or in our understanding of the uniqueness and lordship of Christ, or in our experience with the Holy Spirit. We may have a deficient theology of the body and human sexuality, or we may have misunderstandings in our doctrine of Christian revelation, or our experience of ecclesiology.

We should not dismiss this account because their deficiency is not our deficiency. Rather, we should see this as a centered set whereby we are all moving toward Christ in our journey, and we all have blind spots that we may later look back on regretfully. But the point is that we are on the journey of seeking to come into the full life of what God has for us.

Finally, *Paul places his hands on them to receive the Holy Spirit.* The act of laying on of hands to receive the Spirit is by now familiar to us in the book of Acts. We saw this, for example, with Philip's ministry in Samaria. Even Paul himself, though presumably converted on the road to Damascus, received the Holy Spirit by the laying on of hands several days later through Ananias. One of the persistent points in this book is that we, as Christians, have emphasized the importance of receiving Jesus Christ as our Lord and Savior, but have not had a comparable emphasis on the reception of the Holy Spirit. The early church not only emphasized both, but they actually created two separate liturgical actions or rhythms to mark the events. Water baptism marked the entrance into the faith, the theological space we call justification; and the laying on of hands marked the entrance into the theological space we call sanctification by the Holy Spirit. This, as we have seen, has three dimensions: empowerment for global witness, purifying holiness for sanctified living, and discerning wisdom for life's journey. Power, holiness, and wisdom are just as important from a "big salvation" picture as forgiveness, rebirth, and reconciliation, since both justification and sanctification are subsets of the larger biblical theme of salvation. The Methodist movements distinguished between water baptism and spirit baptism all the way to the nineteenth century, when they began to lose what Wesleyans call the "second half of the gospel." The first half of the gospel refers to the justifying work of Jesus Christ. The second half of the gospel refers to the sanctifying work of the Holy Spirit in the life of the believer. Both are integral to a full reception of the gospel. In other words, God does not just forgive us (justification), he also transforms us and makes us holy (sanctification).

Central to the Christian life should be the recovery of full, biblical Christianity. We have used the phrase "the second half of the gospel" as a shorthand for that. You can call it what you will, but there is a lot of gospel work to be done in our lives and in our churches along these lines. Remember the great trajectory which spilled out over the world through the power of the Holy Spirit. This great, global vision is at the heart of what happens when the Spirit of God infuses his people to join the triune God in his redemptive mission in the world.

Conclusion

In the first century, right in the pages of the New Testament, we discover that the gospel is bigger than Judaism, when a group of unnamed disciples from Cyprus and Cyrene begin to preach the gospel directly to Greeks, as the text says in Acts 11:20, "telling them the good news about the Lord Jesus." The church at Antioch is born, and by the end of the second century becomes the largest church in the world. It was the sending church of the apostle Paul in his great missionary and church-planting journeys. Paul was establishing self-supporting, self-propagating, self-governing churches who themselves began to send out missionaries. This is the story of the church in Cyprus, Pisidian Antioch, Iconium, Lystra, Derbe, Philippi, Thessalonica, Berea, Athens, Corinth, and Ephesus, which forms the backbone of the church expansion in the book of Acts.

By the fourth century, this small persecuted sect became the official faith of the empire, with all the glories and new challenges which that brought. The gospel continued to spread north into the so-called Barbarian territories, and to the far reaches of the empire itself, including a flourishing church in North Africa. The Western church gave us saints like St. Augustine, and the Eastern church, whose capital was now in Constantinople, gave us such leaders as Basil the Great, Gregory of Nazianzus, and John Chrysostom. Later, great Celtic saints like Aidan and Columba and St. Patrick brought the gospel to the western parts of the Europe. And the gospel continued to also spread east across Persia and along the silk route all the way to the Far East. Remarkably, at the same time the gospel was being planted in what is today England, it was also being presented by Nestorian missionaries right into the imperial court of China.

When Islam emerged in the seventh century, Christianity suffered a major setback in North Africa and what we now call the Middle East. Even the Holy Land fell to Islam. But the light of the gospel could not be put out. Boniface brought the gospel into the heart of what is now Germany. Cyril and Methodius were translating the gospel into the Slavic tongue. Vladimir braved the mighty steppes of Russia to bring the gospel. Even in the darkest days of the western attempt to militarily defeat Islam (known as the Crusades), you should not forget that there were faithful bearers of the gospel—men like Raymond Lull, who brought the gospel to the very seat of the Islamic empire. Lull is known as the apostle of love in an age of hate. Eventually, the heart of the gospel message and the authority of the Scripture were recaptured by the

European church in the Reformation of the sixteenth and seventeenth centuries.

The gospel was further recovered in the eighteenth century with George Whitfield, Jonathan Edwards, and the Wesleyan revivals which ushered in the First Great Awakening (1725–1745). Francis Asbury came to the new world as the greatest church planter in the history of our country, and his life connected the First Great Awakening with the Second Great Awakening (1790-1840), which not only gave birth to the holiness movement, but also to the modern missionary movement. In the First Great Awakening, the Moravians streamed forth from the estate of Count von Zinzendorf; and from the Second Great Awakening came the rise of mission societies who sent men and women like William Carey, Adoniram Judson, Hudson Taylor, C. T. Studd, Amy Carmichael, Lottie Moon, Gladys Alyward, and others too numerous to count to the ends of the earth.

The continent of Africa buried missionaries by the hundreds—earning itself the name as "the missionary graveyard" because the average lifespan of a missionary was only two years. But in the end, Christianity took root in the soil of Africa. Today, the fastest-growing church in our day is the African church, and before this century is out, Africa will be the most Christianized continent on the planet.

China called the missionaries foreign devils, but the real story is that the gospel took root in Chinese soil—because the gospel is not Western or Eastern, but is the unfolding global plan of God's redemption for the world. China, by far, has more Christians today than any country in Asia.

In this way the gospel spread all over the world. From the remote islands of the Pacific to the breathtaking mountains of Nepal, this is God's story. From the Jesuit witness in the imperial court of China to the relentless travels of David Livingstone in the heart of Africa—this is God's story. From the work of Wycliffe Bible translators working in the tribal jungles of Papua New Guinea to those working year after year in the great sprawling cities of the Muslim world like Istanbul, Cairo, Damascus, and Jakarta, this is God's story. From new church plants among the immigrant populations of North America to fiery preaching on the streets of Rio or Sao Paulo in South America, this is God's story. From the village evangelists facing persecution in the heat of North India's Ganges plain to the bitter cold winds blowing across the faces of gospel workers in Mongolia, this is God's story. From the mass evangelistic campaigns of Billy Graham to a quiet moment as a young Russian girl kneels at her bedside and, with tears streaming down her cheeks, asks Jesus to save her, this is God's story. From the founding of Asbury Seminary in 1923 to our Seedbed initiative, a twenty-first-century movement and media platform which sows for a great awakening, only eternity will tell the full story. We only know a few of the chapters of this great story of the church of Jesus Christ. But don't you want with every fiber of your being to be a part of this great unfolding story?

We are all moving toward and being summoned by Christ himself to that great day when the strong man is finally disarmed for good, the lepers are cleansed, the lost sons have come home, the great debt is wiped out, the door of the Father's house is flung open wide, the lost sheep are found, the poor and the beggars are seated at the great banquet, the disenfranchised workers have been paid their full wages, the pearl of great price has been unearthed, the bride of Christ has been made spotless. The acceptable year of God's favor has finally come—this is the goal which this grand, Spirit-endowed journey moves us toward. This book has been an invitation to the journey. Let's join it, shall we?

The Holy Spirit's Flame

by Julie Tennent[8]

Tune: Ellacombe (Hosanna, Loud Hosanna)

The Spirit hovered o'er the deep, when first
  creation came;
The Breath of God breathed life in us, who would reflect
    His Name.
To prophesy, to lead and guide, the Spirit was the same;[9]
The Breath of God, beside, within—a holy, living flame.

---

8. One of the traditions associated with these annual books by President Tennent is to include a hymn written particularly for the theme of the book by his wife, Julie.

9. Genesis 1:2; 2:7; Numbers 11:25; Deuteronomy 34:9

In burning bush and guiding fire, God's Spirit called
    with flame;
The fire that passed through broken flesh, His covenant
    proclaimed.
With fire and cloud, Mount Sinai shook, as revelation came;[10]
God's Word and Covenant and Law were all made known
    with flame.

Elijah called down fire to prove the truth of Yahweh's claim;
And Daniel saw a blazing fire when his great vision came.
Isaiah saw the Spirit flow, poured out like water streams;
Ezekiel found dry bones could live, when breath upon
    them came.[11]

With tongues of fire and rushing wind, the Holy Spirit
    came,[12]
On Pentecost the praise of God was pow'rfully proclaimed.
As decades passed the fire still grew, though persecution
    came;
For nothing could prevail against that holy, spreading flame.

---

10. Exodus 3:2; 13:21; Genesis 15:17–18; Exodus 19:16–18
11. 1 Kings 18:24, 37–39; Daniel 7:9–10; Isaiah 44:3; Ezekiel 37:10
12. Acts 2:1–4

In ev'ry great awakening, the gospel is the same;
The spark for true renewal comes alone from that great
    flame.
The cross of Christ that brought us life ignites a blazing
    flame—
The Spirit moves with pow'r to preach when we proclaim
    Christ's name.

The Holy Spirit fills and guides all those who call
    Christ's name;
With wisdom and empowered lives, they will His love
    proclaim.
Though wars and sin and wickedness would put His light
    to shame,
No pow'r of hell can ever quench God's holy spreading
    flame.

Appendix

Being a Spirit-Filled, Sanctified Community

Each year the president of the seminary gives a major address to the entire community at the opening of the academic year. This address was used to begin the 2018–19 academic year and to kick off the sermon series on the Spirit-filled life which is the basis of this book. It was Dr. Timothy C. Tennent's tenth convocation address to the Asbury Seminary community in his role as president of Asbury Theological Seminary.

Each fall, I have sought to focus on different phrases in our mission statement or some aspect of our history or heritage that gave rise to our mission statement. This year, we look at the phrase "sanctified, Spirit-filled."

This is surely one of the most daunting and humbling aspirations that we set forth at the core of our mission. It is not enough, we have said as a community, to graduate students who are theologically educated—as central and important as that is. That is, of course, being done in seminaries all across the world. But, we have also determined that ministry effectiveness must always connect what we know with who we are. Our mission, therefore, is not merely intellectual or cognitive; it is deeply formational. The whole phrase is, "To prepare theologically educated, sanctified, Spirit-filled men and women to evangelize and to spread scriptural holiness throughout the world."

I have gone onto the websites of some of our sister institutions to see what their mission statements say in comparison with ours. This is not intended to be a critique of other institutions' mission statements. I have served joyfully under two of these non-Asbury mission statements. But, a comparison is a helpful way to explore what, if anything, differentiates Asbury Seminary from other institutions, at least in our own missional aspirations.

The mission of Fuller Theological Seminary is "forming global leaders for kingdom vocations." Gordon-Conwell declares that it is "an educational institution serving the Lord and His church. Its mission is to prepare men and women for ministry at home and abroad." Denver Seminary exists to "prepare men and women to engage the needs of the world with the redemptive power of the gospel and the life-changing truth of Scripture."

Trinity Divinity School—part of Trinity International University—declares that their mission is "to educate men and women to engage in God's redemptive work in the world by cultivating academic excellence, Christian faithfulness, and lifelong learning." Reformed Seminary's mission is "to prepare students to serve Christ and His church through biblical, experiential, and practical ministry." Duke Divinity School's mission is "to engage in spiritually disciplined and academically rigorous education in service and witness to the Triune God in the midst of the church, the academy, and the world." Southern Baptist Theological Seminary states that "under the Lordship of Jesus Christ, the mission of the Southern Baptist Theological Seminary is to be totally committed to the Bible as the Word of God, to the Great Commission as our mandate, and to be a servant of the churches of the Southern Baptist Convention by training, educating, and preparing ministers of the gospel for more faithful service."

Those are all beautiful and well-crafted statements. But Asbury Theological Seminary has this remarkable phrase, "sanctified, Spirit-filled." This is a gem for us. I love our mission statement. I could spend ten years expositing all the reasons why I find our mission so compelling. (Oh yeah, I have!) But, for those who may not know my background, I am the first president of Asbury Seminary who had no prior connection whatsoever to Asbury Theological Seminary, Asbury University, or Wilmore, Kentucky. I always loved Asbury from afar, but my first real engaged encounter with the seminary was to read the mission statement. I was a professor at another institution, and I went on the Web, and I typed in "Asbury Theological Seminary mission statement," and it popped up. I was very impressed.

It is such an evangelical and thoroughly Wesleyan statement. I love that it begins with the affirmation of community. We are a community deeply rooted to our heritage, our mission, and to one another. I love the explicit Trinitarian framework of our statement (through the love of Jesus Christ, in the power of the Holy Spirit, to the glory of God the Father). I love that it is framed by the *missio dei*. We are a community "called." It emphasizes God's prior action. With one word it acknowledges that it is God who planted this community, God who calls us forth, and God who ultimately sends us out. Of course, I love the emphasis on theological education, because that is what I have given my life to. I love the historical nod to John Wesley with that great phrase of his "to spread scriptural holiness throughout the land/world." But none of those are the phrases that first captured my attention as I looked at my computer screen years ago and said, "Oh wow!" It was the phrase "sanctified, Spirit-filled." Brothers and sisters, this is what rings out as the distinctive phrase in our mission statement as compared with so many others.

My role as president, among other things, is to assure that we as a seminary are vibrant and moving in the right direction. I oversee our 2023 Strategic Plan. I am responsible to make sure that we are economically viable, and so forth. However, no role of mine is more sacred than guarding and joyfully promoting our mission statement.

Will you, our beloved students, and those who have gone before you, truly go forth to spread scriptural holiness throughout the world? Are you becoming theologically educated? Are you Spirit-filled and sanctified? If you don't know already, every phrase of this is repeated on graduation day, and all graduates are asked to publicly declare that this is exactly what has happened while they were here.

But, is it truly descriptive of who we are, or is it merely aspirational? Let me say it again, the phrase, "sanctified, Spirit-filled" is what sets us apart from the vast majority of the 250 or so other institutions who belong to the Association of Theological Schools. Therefore, it is vital that we as a community never allow the phrase "sanctified,

Spirit-filled" to become mere dead letters, or mere historical markers, which only point to our beloved founders, or some earlier embodiment of our community. Rather, they must continue to be descriptive of who we are and what happens to someone who becomes part of this community of faith and learning. You have not been prepared unless you are becoming both theologically educated and sanctified/Spirit-filled.

I would like to ask two key questions. First, are the words, *sanctified* and *Spirit-filled* redundant expressions, saying the same thing in two ways? In other words, is it kind of like a strophe of Hebrew poetry where parallel phrases are used for beauty and for emphasis, but both carry essentially the same message? If so, we shouldn't try to distinguish greatly between Spirit-filled and sanctified. Or, are the two words capturing different aspects of our Christian experience?

Second, what does it mean for you to be Spirit-filled and sanctified? How do these words or phrases connect with our history and our current practice? What can we do to more fully live into these great missional aspirations?

Let me begin by saying that the two phrases are not redundancies, even if we are not precise about what distinguishes them. Both words were carefully chosen by our founders to say something about the process of discipleship that lies at the heart of Wesleyan identity.

Sanctification as the Grand Depositum

On Wednesday, September 15, 1790, John Wesley wrote a letter to his dear friend, Robert Brakenbury. Brackenbury was a Methodist preacher who established and led the movement in Lincolnshire and was one of Wesley's one hundred top advisors. Wesley wrote him eighteen letters, and the one I want to highlight is his seventeenth. When Wesley wrote this letter, it had been fifty-two years since his famous Aldersgate experience where his heart was "strangely warmed" back in 1738. As Wesley lifts his quill to write his dear friend, he is eighty-seven years old. In six months Wesley would be with the Lord. Let me read you the first part of this letter:

> Dear Sir, your letter gave me great satisfaction. I wanted to hear where and how you were; and am glad to find you are better in bodily health, and not weary and faint in your mind. My body seems to have nearly done its work, and to be almost worn out. Last month my strength was nearly gone, and

I could have sat almost still from morning to night. But, blessed be God, I crept about a bit, and made shift to preach once a day. On Monday I ventured a little farther, and after I had preached three times (once in the open air), I found my strength so restored that I could have preached again without inconvenience. I am glad brother D___ has more light with regard to full sanctification. This doctrine is the grand depositum which God has lodged with the people called Methodists; and for the sake of propagating this chiefly he appeared to have raised us up . . ."

Brothers and sisters, John Wesley is looking back over his entire ministry and this remarkable Methodist movement that God unleashed. Historians would later call this period the Great Awakening. Wesley looks back at this (if I can borrow the phrase from Jonathan Edwards describing these same revivals) "surprising work of God." And Wesley declares that the doctrine of sanctification is the "grand depositum" of what we preach. In fact, he says, it is the very reason that God raised up this movement. This is the great doctrinal deposit (that's what "grand depositum" means) for the people called Methodists.

The sixteenth-century Reformation under the amazing ministries of Luther, Calvin, Zwingli, Knox, Latimer, and all the rest, had restored the doctrine of justification by grace through faith. But, it was the eighteenth century that restored the doctrine of sanctification more fully to the church. It would be a mistake, I think, to assume that Wesley would have said this as clearly in 1738 as he did in 1790. The so-called "grand depositum" was surely the result of what I would call a "grand journey" of the Wesley brothers, and Peter Bohler, and Zinzendorf and Christian David and John Fletcher, and amazing women preachers like Ann Cutler, Sarah Crosby, and Mary Bosanquet—and so many others who were all part of this. They all, despite their differences, gradually realized that the doctrine of sanctification was the grand depositum. This was, in fact, the great contribution of the eighteenth-century revivals to global Christianity.

Of course, all authentically Christian movements embrace the doctrine of sanctification. That is not in question. However, what became increasingly clear to the Wesleys and to those who became co-laborers in this movement, is that the church was debilitated and diminished by equating the word *salvation* with the word *justification*.

As John Wesley and others reexamined the apostolic and patristic writings, they saw that this doctrine had been neglected and had become disconnected from soteriology. Salvation had become reduced to a transactional event, and the longer process of biblical soteriology needed a full recovery. They saw that the church needed to be more intentionally pneumatologically focused—making the shape of our theology more natively triune, as our mission statement also reflects. Compare, for example, some of the classic Reformed systematic theologies such as Henry Thiessen or Louis Berkhof with the Wesleyan theology by Thomas Oden. The former place the Holy Spirit as either a subset of Christology or as a subset of the doctrine of the church. Oden, in contrast, frames his entire three-volume systematic theology around the persons of the triune God.

This grand depositum of sanctification was the holy reminder that the reception of grace is not merely an event, but an ongoing process in the life of the believer. Prevenient grace, justifying grace, sanctifying grace, and finally, in the new creation, glorifying grace, are all part and parcel of a grand, unfolding story of grace and redemption, which was not fully restored in the sixteenth century. We shouldn't be overly critical of the magisterial Reformers on this point. They never claimed that they had completed the Reformation. So, Wesley extends the Reformation. We don't deny total depravity; we just believe that God's grace is greater than our sins.

Ken Collins, in his writings on Wesley, often comments on how Wesleyan theology is optimistic about the capacity of God's grace to transform a person. In other words, we believe that the "yes" of Jesus Christ is greater than the "no" of the devil! We believe that becoming a Christian is not the same as *being* a Christian. We believe that holiness is not an optional accessory for a few, but God's plan for *every* believer. Every single person in this room can be made holy and can live a victorious life in Jesus Christ.

What is quite clear in Wesley's writings and preaching (and, ultimately why the phrase "sanctified, Spirit-filled" eventually found its way into our mission statement) is the belief that there are works of grace, subsequent to justification, which are crucial for your Christian life and the effectiveness of your future ministries. The writings of John Wesley and the hymns of Charles Wesley are filled with many different words to capture this work of grace we call sanctification. I have made a list—by no means comprehensive—of some of the terms that have appeared either in the writings of John Wesley or the hymns of Charles Wesley to describe sanctification: "second blessing," "second gift," "farther grace," "personal Pentecost," "fullness of the Spirit," "Spirit of holiness," "going on to perfection," "baptism with the Holy Spirit," "seal of the Holy Spirit," "effusion of the Spirit," "wrestling Jacob" (from the hymn, "Come O Thou Traveler Unknown"), "inward baptism," and one of my favorites, "uninterrupted holiness." Some may want to argue about the best word for us to use, but the New Testament itself models for us a wide range of terminology for the indwelling empowerment of the Spirit. There is also no precise pattern in which people receive the Spirit. No one makes this point better than Craig Keener in the first of his four-volume commentary on Acts where he says, "Luke allows for a diversity of pneumatic experience and presumably invites his audience to show the same courtesy."[13] So, we are in good company.

But, let me say, brothers and sisters, I don't care what you call it, or even how it happens, just make sure you don't leave here without it! The redirected, sanctified heart is at the core of our message, our identity, and our contribution to global Christianity—don't leave home without it!

---

13. *Acts: An Exegetical Commentary: Introduction and 1:1–2:47* (Baker Academic, 2012).

Being Spirit-Filled

I am indebted to the writings of Larry Wood for pointing out to me that John and Charles Wesley, and several of the other leading writers in the eighteenth-century revivals, relearned from the New Testament and patristic writings that the baptismal liturgy of the early church was a symbolic uniting of Easter with Pentecost. Going into the waters of baptism is, of course, a clear recapitulation of the cross and resurrection, as we die with Christ and are raised with him through the waters of baptism. That is fairly standard across almost all Christian movements. But, what has been often missed, is that baptism was coupled with the laying on of hands to receive the Holy Spirit, which is a recapitulation of Pentecost and the coming of the Holy Spirit. This is why in Acts 19:2 Paul asked, "Did you receive the Holy Spirit when you believed?" It turned out that they only knew John's baptism which was a baptism of repentance, but was not, in fact, the same as Christian baptism. Therefore, they baptized them, and they laid hands on them that they might receive the Holy Spirit. We had already seen this in Acts 6, 8, 9, and 13. In John's gospel, we have Jesus breathing on the disciples and Jesus saying, "Receive the Holy Spirit," demonstrating a coming together of the resurrected Lord with Pentecost in that profound, post-resurrection encounter found only in John's gospel.

John Wesley recovered this, as seen in a letter to William Law when he said, "'baptized with the Holy Spirit' implies this and no more, that we cannot be renewed in righteousness and true holiness any otherwise than by being overshadowed, quickened and animated by the blessed Spirit."[14] We must restore, as part and parcel of our pastoral ministries, the laying on of hands for men and women to receive the Holy Spirit. We must resist with every fiber of our being the noisy gong or clashing cymbal of minimalistic Christianity. We must embrace a full soteriology that is fully Trinitarian and orients believers to both Jesus Christ as our glorious Redeemer, and the Holy Spirit as our blessed Sanctifier.

Five Appropriations of the Holy Spirit in the Lives of Believers

I would like to highlight five major appropriations of the Holy Spirit that we need in our lives. The list could be ten, but I'm going to limit it to five which all arise from the

---

14. *Works*, vol. 9, 495.

New Testament and from our own tradition. This is your test to know if you have been filled with the Holy Spirit. For you new students, this is your first test. Because if you can respond favorably to these five marks, then you are going on to perfection, or whatever else you might call it. And if you cannot, you are not yet sanctified.

First, the Spirit gives us the assurance of our justification. We believe that every believer should have an inner witness of the Spirit that they are a child of God. Wesley is very clear that the moment a person exercises faith in the justifying work of the Son, you should receive a witness of the Spirit that God loves you, that he has pardoned you through the good news of the gospel, and that you exhibit joy and peace through the reconciling work of Christ which is confirmed through the Holy Spirit.[15] This is not only confirmed inwardly in your own heart, but it is confirmed through the community of believers and through the means of grace that you receive in baptism and the Lord's Supper. There is a lot of pastoral work here for you in your future ministries. I cannot tell you how

15. The theme of the role of the Holy Spirit granting assurance is beautifully captured by Keith Getty and Stuart Townend in their hymn, "Resurrection Hymn." The key line is, "through the Spirit who clothes faith with certainty." See *The Asbury Hymnal* (Franklin, TN: Seedbed Publishing, 2018), 92.

many times when I have inquired of one of my parishioners about their spiritual state, some on their death beds, they could only say that they *hoped* that they were going to heaven.

Second, the Spirit grants us bold confidence in the Word of God and we are enabled to proclaim the Word of God boldly. We are experiencing a crisis in the church today of confidence in the Word of God. But the Spirit of God attests to the authority of God's Word. Wesley understood that when you read Scripture, you do not read it alone, but you read in the presence of the risen Christ and through the power of the Holy Spirit. The Spirit inspired the Word of God, and he further enables us to understand it and to appropriate it into our lives. Once understood, we are empowered by the Spirit to preach it and teach it with boldness.

Wesley uses as an example from the text in Acts 4 where the elders and scribes are amazed at the boldness of Peter and John—who after being rebuked, returned to the church and prayed that they might preach the Word of God boldly. Then they were filled with the Spirit, and for the third time in this chapter it states that they spoke the Word of God with boldness. This is repeated in chapter 9:27 with the newly converted Saul of Tarsus, and again in 13:46;

14:3; 18:26; 19:8, 26:26; and 28:31 where Paul and his various companions are said to have preached boldly.

Today, preaching across all of our traditions has become tentative, tepid, fearful, and, at times, almost apologetic. We seem to think that the Word of God is boring and people would rather hear our stories and our opinions than the Word of God. This should be seen as a real sign that we have not been filled with the Holy Spirit with the measure we should be when it comes to our preaching. You can preach a lot of sermons in the flesh, but transformative preaching occurs out of the overflow of the Spirit of God working in you and through you.

Third, the Spirit enables us to live in ever-increasing holiness. The contemporary church has turned discipleship into sin-management programs, without addressing the redirected heart that only happens through an encounter with the Holy Spirit that is just as real as the encounter we insist one must have with Jesus Christ. If you are struggling with persistent or recurring sin in your life, you need to be filled and keep on being filled with the Holy Spirit.

This comes to us both as an event, as well as process and appropriation. We need clear moments where the triune God acts and fills us with the Spirit—through the laying on of hands—that is an event. But, we also need ongoing growth through disciplined membership in band meetings—that is a process. This is why, I believe, our mission statement distinguishes between Spirit-filled and sanctified—because we can be filled with the Holy Spirit, and yet we continue to need more of the Holy Spirit as we move toward full sanctification. The terms are not interchangeable. "Be filled with the Holy Spirit" is both a command and an ongoing process. Pentecost is not like the resurrection. It is not a one-time event, but one that happens over and over again in the book of Acts. The early church kept getting filled with the Holy Spirit, even as they were "going on to perfection" with the goal of entire sanctification. Both are event and process, but the purpose of being filled with the Spirit is so that you might be sanctified.

I exhort every student—indeed, everyone at Asbury Theological Seminary—staff, faculty, administration, students, everyone—to be part of a band meeting. Kevin Watson's book *The Band Meeting*[16] is probably the best introduction to the nuts-and-bolts of being part of a band if you need more guidance. Seedbed has a special

---

16. Kevin Watson and Scott Kisker, *The Band Meeting: Rediscovering Relational Discipleship in Transformational Community* (Franklin, TN: Seedbed Publishing, 2017).

app—Band Together—which is dedicated to helping facilitate band meetings.

The fruit of the Spirit should also be manifest in our community in an ever-increasing way. We live in a culture that has become degraded and crude. We live in a culture that is shockingly deficient in love, joy, peace, patience, kindness, goodness, gentleness, faithfulness, and self-control. Therefore, to bear this fruit is to shine like bright lights in a culture filled with hatred, sadness, warfare, profanity, anxiety, impatience, crudeness, faithlessness, and being out of control—the anti-fruits of the Spirit, or the fruit of the flesh. We want to see the end of all bondages to sin in our community, whether it be pornography or gaming addictions or opioid use, or drunkenness, or hating your body, or shaming, or any other signs of brokenness that would creep into our community.

We also joyfully recognize the gifts of the Spirit as available to the church through all time. I am indebted to Thomas Oden for setting forth so clearly in his multi-volume work on Wesley's theology, that John Wesley established a clear *via media* between, on the one hand, a cold, rationalistic kind of Christianity which was closer to Deism than it was the New Testament and, on the other hand, emotional extremism that is focused more on experience than on the cultivation of holiness. Properly ordered, Wesley believed that the gifts of the Spirit should be fully operational in a truly renewed church, as his lengthy letter to the skeptic Conyers Middleton makes abundantly clear. In fact, Wesley even envisioned a church whereby a dead person could be raised up or demons be cast out, experiences foreign to much of our Western contemporary Christian experience.

Fourth, the Spirit calls us to be agents of societal transformation. We reject a truncated, post-Enlightenment form of the gospel that turns the whole enterprise into a privatized faith disconnected from the world we live in. The modern world is content with our being Christian as long as we keep it in our heads as nothing more than personal preference. The New Testament understands that holiness has implications that are personal as well as societal and structural. The church is helping to foster the in-breaking kingdom when we work for justice for the poor, hope for the disenfranchised, and desperately needed racial reconciliation. The church celebrates recovery for addicts and mercy to the immigrants. The church holds up truth in morality and righteousness in a culture that has lost its way. There is no part of creation that we do not work to see under the lordship of Jesus Christ, as we become his co-laborers in reaching the world! Does your heart ache for all this?

Fifth, the Spirit empowers us to bring the gospel to the ends of the earth—to "spread scriptural holiness throughout the world." We are those who are burdened—our hearts burn like fire—for those who have never heard the gospel of Jesus Christ. Indeed, this is the primary function of the Spirit in Acts; namely, to witness to the nations. There are thousands of people groups in the world with no gospel witness and no one to bring them the gospel unless the church acts. There are thousands of biblical nations (i.e., ethnic people groups) with not even John 3:16 translated into their language. There is an entire rising generation of young people in this country who have no Christian memory.

Brothers and sisters at Asbury Theological Seminary, we are called to go into all the world precisely because God's prevenient grace has already beat us there. That prevenient grace becomes embodied in modern flesh-and-blood versions of the Macedonian Man who continues to call and beckon us to new places of ministry.

Conclusion

When H. C. Morrison founded Asbury Theological Seminary in 1923, he called this community to be sanctified and Spirit-filled. To be Spirit-filled and sanctified is not some sectarian doctrine, but is at the heart of the gospel "once for all delivered to the saints." This is basic *Scriptural Christianity.* Scriptural Christianity is what the early apologists defended in the second century. This is why Athanasius wouldn't budge as he fought the Arian heresy in the third century. This is the legacy of the Cappadocian fathers in the fourth century. This is at the heart of Aquinas's *Summa Theologica* in the thirteenth century. This is part of the Puritan and Pietistic struggle of the seventeenth century. This is Wesley's "grand depositum" of the eighteenth century.

The mantle has now passed to us. It is now our turn to keep remembering the faith. Let us not believe too small, or be found with tiny prayers, stunted faith, or powerless lives. Let us not lose our courage when it comes to standing in the truth of the Word of God. Let us embrace with boldness the full inheritance that is ours through the full ministry of the triune God. May each of us be Spirit-filled and sanctified. Amen.